With Wit and Wonder

With Wit and Wonder

The Preacher's Use of Humour and Imagination

BLAYNE A. BANTING

RESOURCE *Publications* • Eugene, Oregon

WITH WIT AND WONDER
The Preacher's Use of Humour and Imagination

Copyright © 2013 Blayne A. Banting. All rights reserved. Except for brief quotations in critical publications or reviews, no part of this book may be reproduced in any manner without prior written permission from the publisher. Write: Permissions. Wipf and Stock Publishers, 199 W. 8th Ave., Suite 3, Eugene, OR 97401.

Resource Publications
An Imprint of Wipf and Stock Publishers
199 W. 8th Ave., Suite 3
Eugene, OR 97401

www.wipfandstock.com

ISBN 13: 978-1-62032-796-8

Manufactured in the U.S.A.

This book is dedicated to all the witty and wonderful church members in Nanton, AB, Calgary, AB, Yellow Grass, SK, Charlottetown, PE and Caronport, SK who have persevered through my stumbling attempts at wit and wonder as their preacher. Special mention goes to those who have sat around our dinner table and had to endure this daily – to a loving wife and four forgiving children.

Contents

Foreword by Phil Callaway ix

Introduction: Why Wit and Wonder? 1

1 | A "Theolory" of Wit 18
2 | A "Theolory" of Wonder 46
3 | The Use of Wit in Sermon Development 67
4 | The Use of Wonder in Sermon Development 94
5 | Wit and Wonder in Sermon Delivery 119

Appendix A: Forms of Humour 131
Appendix B: Definitions of Wonder 134
Appendix C: Comparison of Left-Mode and Right-Mode Characteristics of the Brain 137

Bibliography 139

Foreword
—Phil Callaway

I LOVE THE TOPIC and content of the book you are holding. Blayne Banting is practical, non-stuffy, imaginative, wise, and borderline witty. He's the kind of guy I listen to because he lives what he writes. Plus he's a ton of fun to exchange emails with.

I once asked Chuck Swindoll what he takes the most heat for. "My sense of humor," he replied. Surprising, isn't it? Yet I would agree. Few things have dipped me in more hot water than my wit. This is to be expected if laughs were gained at the expense of my wife or my humor was rooted in the compost of most comedy clubs. But I've come to realize that laughter is a sacred gift. When Christians laugh, the enemy doesn't. When Christians laugh, the world takes notice. Laughter is one of the most underused, underrated and powerful witnessing tools we as ministers have. And anything this sacred and effective will draw fire. When I asked Chuck why he takes heat for humor, he said, "Some people want you to be as miserable as they are and I'm not getting on that bus."

Amen.

I was speaking to four hundred women in Niagara Falls. Not in the falls, but at a nearby hotel. On the Sunday morning a gentleman sneaked in and sat at the back. Afterward, he eagerly told me that he played in the hotel bar band. They rocked the joint until two in morning, but he woke early and couldn't sleep. Wandering about the lobby, he heard women laughing and tiptoed in. "I couldn't believe you were followers of Jesus," he said. "Laughing!

Foreword

Imagine!" Holding up a sheet of paper, he showed me that he'd been taking notes, writing down Scripture references and quotes from Jesus. Then the tears came. "My parents have been praying for me for years," he said. "Their prayers were answered this morning. I'm finally home."

In that talk I had simply done with humor, warmth, and imagination what Blayne advocates in this book.

In Galatians 4:15 Paul asks a church that has strayed far from God, "What has happened to all your joy?" We've all been in churches like that. Sad places where the only fruit of the Spirit that seems evident is prunes. Nowhere does the Bible advocate long-faced Christianity. God is a God of joy. Let's bring it back.

In Acts 14 we read that God showed himself in three ways: He gave rain from heaven, provided food, and filled their hearts with joy. He has done the same for us. And we long to share this with others. If you'd like to join a long line of great preachers (including Charles Spurgeon and Oswald Chambers) who were criticized for their humor, read on. If you'd like to see lives changed and filled with joy, laugh on too. You never know who's listening.

Introduction
Why Wit and Wonder?

YOUR HEAD MAY BE swirling with a check list of questions: "Why should I take time from my busy ministry schedule to read a book about developing my sense of humour and imagination?" "Why humour and imagination—how are they even connected to each other?" "Why bother with all this funny and frivolous stuff when I'm a man of left-brained lips and I dwell among a people of left-brained lips?" "Are you suggesting I'm not supposed to take my faith and ministry seriously?" "Can I use humour and imagination in my ministry when both of them can have some rather inappropriate expressions?" "I'm already struggling to keep afloat in all the tasks and expectations of my ministry; why should I take time to read about something that will not have a practical payoff?" The list could go on, I'm sure, but these are good for a start. As a full-time pastor and part-time professor, I share many of these same concerns and have empathy for the time pressures that are part of today's pastoral life. So let me try to put your mind at ease and demonstrate why wit and wonder might just become your new best friends over these next pages. When the dust has cleared, I hope to be able to help you put the "u" in humour and the "I" in imagination. If you didn't "get" that rather pathetic attempt at humour, it might take longer than I thought (for both of us). Check your ministry schedule. Do you have a minute . . . or two?

Another thing—I have made up my mind to adopt a style in this book that is part way between a stuffy, academic approach and one that is downright informal and chatty. This usually pleases no one, but I have my reasons. For those who are looking for a more erudite approach, it might help to know I have written a doctoral thesis on humour and had one of my thesis readers remark during my oral defense, "For a thesis on humour, this really isn't very funny." So I suppose I could do that again, but would rather not. If you would prefer a book like that, try checking out some of the ones I have listed in the Bibliography at the end of this book. You can thank me later. Some of you may be looking for a quick, magical fix and want to be funnier and more creative yesterday. That's not going to happen either. You probably should be watching video clips and reading blogs and not bother with a book at all. Besides, you will find out I think it is just as important to figure out *why* you want to be funny and creative as it is to know *how*. So there might be too much theory and theology for you, I'm guessing. Sorry.

One more confession before we proceed. In the past, I was guilty of thinking both humour and imagination were icing on the cake—the cream cheese you added to the cake to keep people from realizing it was made of carrots or zucchini. This can lead to a very utilitarian view of what God has given us as the very essence of our lives. Humour and imagination are not to be smeared on top or merely poured over what we preach, they are essential parts of the process itself. They are not attractive accessories to dress up our dull sermons or other creations—they are part of what is means to create anything. Humour and imagination are gifts given to us from our Creator, evidences that we bear the image of One who spoke all things into being and who has committed to us a story that literally vibrates with pathos, comedy, creativity, and diversity. On top of that, the ministry contexts in which we are called to preach this story call for every ounce of the creative juices that is within us.

So if you are still with me, let me begin with an apologetic for wit and wonder. It's important to know what I mean and don't mean by these two terms (in case it isn't obvious, I'm using "wit" and "humour" as synonyms and use "wonder" and "imagination" the same way), since both of them are open to a wide range of interpretation. I will define both humour and imagination in detail in

Introduction

the following chapters, so let's concern ourselves with some of the broader issues first.

WHY BOTH WIT AND WONDER?

What is it that humour and imagination share in common that allows me to treat them in close relation to each other? Obviously, they are not identical. Some humorous people are not very imaginative and some imaginative people are hardly what you would call funny. Not everything we would call imaginative would qualify as humorous and vice versa. So why connect the two?

Both humour and imagination come from the same approach to perception and thought. Humour theorist Arthur Koestler maintains that humour, scientific discovery and art all employ bisociative thought. In other words, the jester, the sage and the artist all have something in common—they all employ the same type of thought but towards different ends. Koestler states: "The bisociative act connects previously unconnected matrices of experience; it makes us 'understand what it is to be awake, to be living on several planes at once. . . .'[1] The contrast here is with what Koestler calls "associative" thought (or what might be termed "analytical" or "reasonable" thought processes):

> The skills of reasoning rely on habit, governed by well-established rules of the game; the 'reasonable person'—used as a standard norm in English common law—is level-headed instead of multi-level-headed; adaptive and not destructive; an enlightened conservative, not a revolutionary; willing to learn under proper guidance, but unable to be guided by his dreams.[2]

Koestler makes the connection between humour, discovery and art by showing how each employs bisociative acts to connect these "previously unconnected matrices of experience": "When two independent matrices of perception or reasoning interact with each other the result . . . is either a *collision* ending in laughter, or their

1. Koestler, *The Act of Creation*, 45.
2. Ibid., 659.

fusion in a new intellectual synthesis [i.e. discovery], or their *confrontation* in an aesthetic experience [italics his]."³

All of this to say, a humorous perspective and an imaginative perception are related by the same basic kind of thought process. Instead of thinking in well-worn norms, both humour and imagination require thought processes that intentionally stray from these ruts in order to find some previously undiscovered connection between "unconnected" realities. Rather than thought processes that only go backwards (arguing from axiom to implication—or deductive thought) and forwards (from particulars to hypotheses—or inductive thought), humour and imagination call on us to think "sideways" (more on that in a later chapter). So, no matter what you call this thought process—synthetic, intuitive, right-brained, generative, lateral, divergent, etc.—it helps us with both our humorous and imaginative perception. Hopefully, this is not too confusing. I promise it will make more sense as we move along. Remember . . . you asked!

POSSIBLE RESERVATIONS

What about the many inappropriate expressions of both humour and creative imagination that are hardly fodder for any preacher's repertoire? There is no denying that much that is termed either humorous or imaginative today hardly glorifies God. So my encouragement to you in developing your humorous and imaginative capacities must have some limitations. Don't worry—my goal is not to have you stand up in front of your congregation and perform either like some off-color stand-up comic or a suggestive performance artist! I will try to give a voice to some of your possible reservations about wit and wonder and at the same time establish some needed limitations and qualifications for humour and imagination that honors God. To help give shape to this discussion, I appeal to two well-respected preachers: John Stott and Haddon Robinson. These two men have trained a generation of preachers and have helped us by noting that all preachers live in at least four different

3. Ibid., 45.

Introduction

worlds: the world of the biblical text, the contemporary world, the personal world of the preacher and the world of the particular context in which the preacher serves.[4] These four worlds will give shape to our treatment of your possible reservations.

The World of the Biblical Text

At first glance, at least, there seems to be little that is witty or whimsical about the Christian Scriptures. The Bible addresses matters of eternal consequence, including the fall of humanity, the cross of Christ and impending judgment. For that reason, historically the Christian church has approached Scripture with an appropriate sense of serious reverence. There is certainly nothing wrong with that. What I am promoting on behalf of wit and wonder is not designed to compete with a sense of fear and trembling before the biblical text, but rather to complement it. What I will be arguing here is that a "serious" treatment of any biblical text will involve a playful engagement as well as a reverent one because both are evident within Scripture itself. I'm not even arguing for the primacy of wit and wonder, just a place for them at the exegetical table. The issue has always been one of balance and so far the scales have been weighted heavily in favor of a rather somber approach. On one occasion Zen philosopher D.T. Suzuki facetiously summed up our faith by saying, "God against man. Man against God. Man against nature. Nature against man. Nature against God. God against nature—very funny religion."[5] We bristle against this unfair caricature of the Christian faith but maybe we have been unwitting (pardon the pun) participants in giving this impression to a watching world. For centuries the church has betrayed an unhealthy imbalance toward pietistic asceticism and rationalistic scholasticism. It is this imbalance that needs to addressed, not the need for proper sober mindedness itself.

---

4. Mead, "World Four," *Biblical Preaching* (blog), August 29, 2007, http://wordpress.com/world-four.

5. Nilson, *Humor Scholarship*, 233.

So I will list a few possible reservations regarding wit and wonder that come from the world of the biblical text and hopefully address them to your satisfaction. Each of these will contribute to a fuller picture of the role of humour and imagination rightly conceived within the ministry of preaching.

Laughter in the Bible.

Is it not true that most of the occasions where laughter is mentioned in the Bible are ones that mock or deride someone or something? That is true, but that hardly would bring a blanket prohibition against anything humorous, for several reasons. First, it is important not to equate humour with laughter. They are related but are not the same. Humour deals with certain qualities within a statement or experience and laughter is only one way of responding to that humour. We can respond to something humorous in ways other than laughter. Also there are many experiences that elicit laughter that are hardly funny. There are anxious and even psychotic forms of laughter. So, technically speaking, laughter should not be equated with humour.

Even so, recognizing that humour and laughter are often related, we need to point out the redemptive uses of laughter found in Scripture. We note that Jesus speaks of laughter as an expression of eschatological joy in Luke 6:21b: "Blessed are you who weep now, for you shall laugh." Sarah's famous incredulous laughter when hearing the prediction of her giving birth in her old age (Gen 18:12) is redeemed after the birth of Isaac (whose name means "he laughs"): "God has made laughter for me; everyone who hears will laugh over me" (Gen 21:6). It is important to recognize these positive uses of laughter so our understanding is accurate and balanced.

Prohibitions of Frivolity.

Aren't there many biblical texts that prohibit frivolous behavior and encourage sober mindedness? We could note the constant censure of the "fool" in wisdom literature as well as many pointed texts

Introduction

which may dampen our enthusiasm for a sense of playfulness in our faith. Here's at least a partial list of these from the New Testament:

> "Woe to you who laugh now, for you shall mourn and weep" (Luke 6:25b)
>
> "Let no corrupting talk come out of your mouths, but only such as is good for building up, as fits the occasion, that it may give grace to those who hear" (Eph 4:29)
>
> "Let there be no filthiness nor foolish talk nor crude joking, which are out of place, but instead let there be thanksgiving" (Eph 5:4)
>
> "But now you must put them all away: anger, wrath, malice, slander and obscene talk from your mouth" (Col 3:8)
>
> "So then let us not sleep, but let us keep awake and be sober. For those who sleep, sleep at night, and those who get drunk, are drunk at night. But since we belong to the day, let us be sober, having put on the breastplate of faith and love, and for a helmet the hope of salvation" (1 Thess 5:6–8)
>
> "O Timothy, guard the deposit entrusted to you. Avoid the irreverent babble and contradictions of what is falsely called "knowledge"'" (1 Tim 6:20)
>
> "But avoid irreverent babble, for it will lead people into more and more ungodliness" (2 Tim 2:16)
>
> "Show yourself in all respects to be a model of good works and in your teaching show integrity, dignity, and sound speech that cannot be condemned, so that an opponent may be put to shame, having nothing evil to say about us" (Titus 2:7, 8)
>
> "Be wretched and mourn and weep. Let your laughter be turned to mourning and your joy to gloom" (Jas 4:9).

This is a sobering list! At this point, all I need to say is that the wit and wonder I propose is not the kind rightly condemned in the above texts. The frivolity prohibited in these texts comes from a rebellious and immoral life that is opposed to the new life given to

7

believers in the gospel of Christ. Rest assured the levity I propose does not ignore the gravity necessary in matters of obedience to Christ. We can be creative and funny without being frivolous.

Jesus Didn't Laugh.

The gospel writers record instances where Jesus commands, commends, condemns, warns, exorcises, weeps and even times when he is amazed. Nowhere in the gospels does it record that Jesus laughed. John Chrysostom (444/45–507 AD) apparently thought this fact was a big deal:

> If you also weep such tears, you have become a follower of your Lord. For he too wept, both over Lazarus and over the city, and he was deeply moved over the fate of Judas. And this indeed may one often see him do, but nowhere laugh or smile even a little, no one at least of the evangelists mentions this. . . . That is why Christ says so much to us about mourning, and blesses those who mourn, and calls those who laugh wretched. For this is not the theatre for laughter, neither did we come together for this intent, that we may give way to immoderate mirth, but that we may groan, and by this groaning inherit a kingdom.[6]

While I can sympathize with Chrysostom, especially given his time and his context, his understanding of Jesus' message hardly sounds like "good" news. He also uses an argument from silence which is hardly convincing—the gospels don't mention that Jesus coughed either. Besides, Luke records that Jesus "rejoiced in the Holy Spirit" (10:21) which may not be laughter exactly, but is close enough to poke a hole in Chrysostom's argument. We need to remember our need for balance here as well as the fact that laughter is not identical to wit or wonder. The issue becomes not whether Jesus laughed or not, but whether he employed humour—and that is indeed the case as I will demonstrate later. It might be helpful to remember

---

6. John Chrysostom, *Homilies on the Gospel of Matthew*. Post Nicene Christian Library, *Homily VI.6* quoted in Kuschel, *Laughter*, 46, 47.

Introduction

G.K. Chesterton's comment: "There was some one thing that was too great for God to show us when he walked upon the earth; and I have sometimes fancied that it was his mirth."

Prohibitions Against Imagination.

Are there not biblical texts which condemn the products of human minds as rebellious, vain and idolatrous? Again, we could compile a list. There are numerous texts which condemn and even lampoon (am I tipping my hand here?) the making of idols which are the result of human creative efforts but express a rebellious spirit. Here are a few New Testament texts which might suggest that the result of human imagination has ominous consequences:

> "And I, when I came to you, brothers, did not come proclaiming to you the testimony of God with lofty speech or wisdom. For I decided to know nothing among you except Jesus Christ and him crucified. And I was with you in weakness and in fear and much trembling, and my speech and my message were not in plausible words of wisdom, but in demonstration of the Spirit and of power, that your faith might not rest in the wisdom of men but in the power of God" (1 Cor 2:1-5)
>
> "See to it that no one takes you captive by philosophy and empty deceit, according to human tradition, according to the elemental spirits of the world, and not according to Christ" (Col 2:8)
>
> "Have nothing to do with irreverent silly myths. Rather train yourself for godliness" (1 Tim 4:7)
>
> "Have nothing to do with foolish, ignorant controversies; you know that they breed quarrels" (2 Tim 2:23)
>
> "For the time is coming when people will not endure sound teaching, but having itching ears they will accumulate for themselves teachers to suit their own passions, and will turn away from listening to the truth and wander off into myths. As for you, always be sober-minded,

> endure suffering, do the work of an evangelist, fulfill your ministry" (2 Tim 4:3–5)
>
> "This testimony is true [regarding the Cretans]. Therefore rebuke them sharply, that they may be sound in the faith, not devoting themselves to Jewish myths and the commands of people who turn away from the truth" (Titus 1:13, 14)

It should be obvious enough that these texts do not prohibit the use of imagination in the way I propose it, but the warnings stem from some erroneous sermonic treatments of these texts. Not every product of the human imagination is rebellious and idolatrous—some contribute to our worship and obedience to Christ. A.W. Tozer weighs in here:

> That the imagination is of great value in the service of God may be denied by some persons who have erroneously confused the word "imaginative" with the word "imaginary." The gospel of Jesus Christ has no truck with things imaginary. The most realistic book in the world is the Bible. God is real, men are real and so is sin and so are death and hell, toward which sin inevitable leads. The presence of God is not imaginary, neither is prayer the indulgence of a delightful fancy. The objects that engage the praying man's attention, while not material, are nevertheless completely real; more certainly real, it will at last be admitted, than any earthly object. The value of the cleansed imagination in the sphere of religion lies in its power to perceive in natural things shadows of things spiritual.[7]

The Contemporary World

Our discomfort with wit and wonder might come from ways in which they often are employed in our contemporary context. You might be concerned, among other things, with the basic nature of

---

7. Tozer, "The Value of a Sanctified Imagination," 212, 213.

Introduction

humour and imagination these days or with the lifestyles that seem to accompany them, or both. We'll take a look at both of these first.

The Contemporary Nature of Wit and Wisdom.

You may be observing the devolution of humour and creative imagination in contemporary media and wonder if it knows no bounds. There seems to be a cynical and antagonistic spirit evident in much of what we see and hear these days. I don't need to belabor the point with documentation—there are enough evidences found on every screen, printed page and stage. We are to be legitimately concerned about the effect this has on all of us. Do we really want to emulate this edgy, flippant, frivolous, nihilistic, crude, and Bohemian attitude in our pulpits? That is obviously a rhetorical question!

Much of this comes from the spirit of our times. Postmodernity has successfully dismantled many of the taboos that have kept chaos at bay for centuries. We've all been invited to a sacred cow barbeque. There seems to be nothing that is above criticism or mockery. With meaning as the first victim of this mindset, everything is now fodder for ridicule or replacement. Now everything can be funny and nothing needs to be taken seriously. But in a world where everything is funny, nothing is funny. Some of this recent descent into deconstruction is really a symptom of despair. That is not to say some our cherished taboos weren't ripe for ridicule. Some of what we have lost, needed to be tossed. Some of our taboos were more vestiges of spiritual constipation or of a Victorian type of Stoicism that blushed at the Bible's honesty about our condition rather than promoting a full-bodied Christian spirituality. So there is reason for deep concern but not all is lost. Keep your white flag in your pocket because it's not over just yet. What I suggest is not wit and wisdom that have caved in to the contemporary cynical spirit, but that bring an honest and redemptive perspective to both a crotchety conservatism and an angry agnosticism. Wit and wisdom do not have to be flippant, crude, nihilistic, cynical, antagonistic, relativistic or hedonistic but can be positively iconoclastic and subversive, playful, comical, generative and "wonder"ful in the best senses of these terms. Theologian Conrad Hyers would agree—humour is not purely deconstructive but constructive as well. He notes, "Comedy presupposes some frame of reference, some article of faith, some vision of hope, some sense of mystery that has not been reduced to an absurdist credo."[8]

Lifestyles of the Funny and Frivolous.

Your reservations may come from your knowledge of the hedonistic lifestyles of those heralded as witty and creative in our culture. No doubt aided by the growing cult of celebrity, we now know more than we should about the lives of these luminaries. Much of what we hear and see suggests that all kinds of self-absorbed behaviors come along with the life of a comic or an artist. Doesn't this necessarily taint our use of humour and imagination? Granted, we're all fallen creatures and this could happen to us but it doesn't have to. The temptation does not inevitably lead to adopting this kind of excess. Part of the problem, of course, is the mad media frenzy that surrounds these celebrities. The result is they indeed become larger than life and give the false impression that everyone who is witty or creative must live this way. Again the last word belongs to A.W. Tozer:

> The imagination, since it is a faculty of the natural mind, must necessarily suffer both from its intrinsic limitations and from an inherent bent toward evil. . . . A purified and Spirit-controlled imagination is, however, quite another thing, and it is this I have in mind here. I long to see the imagination released from its prison and given to its proper place among the sons of the new creation. What I am trying to describe here is a sacred gift of seeing, the ability to peer beyond the veil and gaze with astonished wonder upon the beauties and mysteries of things holy and eternal.[9]

---

8. Hyers, *The Comic Vision and the Christian Faith*, 167.
9. Tozer, "The Value of a Sanctified Imagination," 213, 214.

Introduction

The Dumbing Down of Creativity in the Contemporary World.

Maybe your issue with the world we live in is not shock and awe about how wildly out of control things are due to lack of controls on excessive and aggressive forms of creativity. Maybe you have the opposite concern that our contemporary culture has done more to stultify creativity than to allow it to run amok. Either way, there is reason for concern. With all our electronic gizmos and gadgets, with the world at our very fingertips, you would think we would be the most creative of all generations. That is simply not the case. Pundits warn us repeatedly that levels of creativity within the general North American population are decreasing rather than increasing. The last two decades have seen a steady dip in the average North American's capacity to be creative and think outside the box. There are all kinds of scapegoats for this trend. The most commonly cited are: increased emphasis upon productivity over creativity, harried lifestyles which allow no time for creative reflection, increasing passivity in watching screens rather than getting actively involved, once-size-fits-all approaches to education that fail to inspire many students, and the preference of movies over books where the video is supplied rather than imagined actively by the reader. These factors have caused widespread atrophy in our ability to imagine and create. Attention spans decrease, creativity levels decrease.

As one who preaches regularly to this kind of audience, are you concerned how you will keep their attention, grip their minds and inspire their imaginations? Is it really all that creative to show the latest video clip in your sermon in a desperate attempt to be relevant or hip? What about you? Are you tempted, with all the other tasks crowding your calendar, to cut corners and download something attractive from the web that has been used by someone else to rave reviews? Here is where preachers can be proactive and model positive uses of wit and wisdom as a good example to congregants who would normally just sit there hoping to be entertained. Understanding wit and wisdom can actually help to activate your passive pew potatoes into ones who love God and follow Jesus with all their heart, soul, mind and strength.

The Personal World of the Preacher

Your issue with wit and wonder might stem from your struggle with your own capacity to employ them profitably in your preaching ministry. You might protest, "I'm just not funny or creative and when I try to be, it only makes it worse." There is the debate between nature and nurture and both sides make their points, but neither side wins by a landslide. Are you born with a sense of humour or can you develop one? Are creative people *born* or *made*? I would say creative people are *born to be made*. There may be some innate factors that come into play, but anyone can become more witty and imaginative. Granted, there are some to whom this comes more naturally, but we all can share at least a small piece of this pie.

A Word to the Witty and Imaginative Preacher.

Maybe you have been blessed with a capacity to look at life in a way that sparkles with wit and creative insight. That puts you in the minority. Most of us are not blessed with those gifts to begin with. Let me offer a few suggestions so this blessing does not become a burden either to you or your congregation.

It is possible to get too much of a good thing. Ask anyone who works in a chocolate factory. The greatest temptation for the witty and creative preacher is to over-use those gifts so that they take center stage and the truth of the gospel ends up playing second or third fiddle. These gifts are means to a greater end and not the end themselves. If they become the master, they quickly turn on us and force us to up the ante every time until we go way beyond the boundaries of our gift or good taste or both. This can become a candy-coated addiction, similar to the stand-up comic who begins to live for the laugh. Sometimes when you get on a roll, it's hard to put on the brakes, the adrenaline rush is intoxicating. But remember why you're there. The preacher's job is to announce the good news and not draw attention to the way that is done. We're not called to make the pizza, just to deliver it. On those occasions when you feel like you're on a roll and it's getting out of control, bounce your ideas off someone who loves you and your congregation enough to tell you

Introduction

when enough is enough. My "go to" person is my wife who serves as my "stupid filter" and tells me when my idea is either stupid or harmful or both. May their tribe increase!

A Word to the Wit and Wonder Impaired.

The majority of us struggle with ways to increase our sense of humour and creativity, not to rein it in. So if you are looking for ways to enhance your capacity to employ humour and imagination, here are a few suggestions:

1. Determine your wit and wonder style. Ask those closest to you how they would describe your style of wit and wonder. Look for repeated themes and then begin to investigate the types of humour and creativity that seem most natural to you. Do a search on the internet for assessment instruments that can help you with your aptitudes in humour and creativity. You might want to try one of the more general assessment instruments like the Myers-Briggs Type Indicator or the DISC instrument. There is a considerable amount of research surrounding both of these instruments, especially the MBTI, and you can gain helpful tips as to your wit and wonder preferences. And don't worry if your MBTI profile has a high "J" (i.e. judging); there is hope for you yet!

2. Spend time with children. Children are brutally honest and wonderfully free to explore almost anything—even if it doesn't make sense. Part of our problem as adults is we have given up the playful attitude of children because we feel it is irresponsible now that we're all grown up. We tend to get boring with age. Why should that have to be the case? Maybe a child should lead us—that almost sounds biblical, doesn't it? Why not try to follow their lead by trying something out of your normal comfort zone? Hanging out with children will show you how. You might want to try this first in a place where you are relatively anonymous until you grow more comfortable with this sort of thing (just sayin').

3. Look for wit and wonder in the mundane. Train yourself to

look at life in such a way that you see the incongruities and possibilities for creativity and humour. Funny and creative people inhabit the same universe we do. They look at the same scenery we do but in a different way. Try looking at experiences from another perspective. The next time you see a person walking a dog, try to imagine the same scene through the eyes of the dog. Does anything pop?

4. Spend time with humorous and imaginative people. Wit and wonder are contagious—maybe not as much as the flu but if you spend enough time with them, you will catch the bug. Much learning and growth takes place within social interaction. We can spur each other on toward wit and good wonder. Creative juices often begin to flow when you're in a crowd that encourages growth and risk while offering support and acceptance. You may actually find as much reward in helping others to experiment as you do in your own development.

5. Give your mind a steady diet of wit and wonder. Try to discipline yourself to read material that is humorous and imaginative. Spend time listening to creative and funny people on television and in theatres. This would include good story tellers, stand-up comics, and poets. Don't ignore television commercials. Companies have a few seconds to get your attention and trigger a response. Often they use humour and creativity to do so. The more you become conversant with these qualities, the more they become obvious to you. You also will find your ability to notice humour and creativity increasing as you read the Bible (more on that later).

The World of the Congregational Context.

Your final reservations might relate to the actual place where you preach on a regular basis. Obviously every congregational context is unique. What will fly in one place will crash and burn in another. There are even differences within the same congregational context. There are certain times when the expectations and the receptivity regarding humour and imagination change even within the same

Introduction

congregation. Your manner automatically changes from performing a funeral to speaking to the youth group in a retreat setting. Morning services and evening services (remember those?) can have their own unique ethos.

With all this said, there are a few factors to note in determining appropriate approaches to wit and wonder in your congregational setting. Take special note of your congregation's demographics (age, race, gender, socio-economic level, educational level, geography, spiritual maturity, etc.). What was your predecessor's style (If he/she was loved, take heed; if he/she was not, take warning)? How were your own examples of wit and wonder received by the congregation in the past? If there is too great a change in too short a time period, the congregation may wonder if you've lost your wits.

After all this, the book is only beginning. Hopefully I've convinced you of the merit of enhancing your capacities in wit and wonder. In the first two chapters I will attempt to lay a theoretical and theological foundation for wit and wonder. Chapter 1 deals with the "theolory" of wit (don't bother looking up "theolory" in a dictionary—I just made it up by combining 'theology' and 'theory'). Chapter 2 will deal with the "theolory" of wonder. These two chapters may require you to do a little heavy lifting, but don't give in to the temptation to skip over them. You'll be quizzed on them later (just kidding!). Chapters 3 and 4 respectively will address the use of humour and imagination in sermon development. These chapters are more related to the practice of preaching itself. Chapter 5 will deal with how wit and wonder might be used in sermon delivery. This chapter includes some ideas you might want to try or ones that might spur you on to flex your own wit and wonder muscles.

1 | A "Theolory" of Wit

No, that is not a typo. For those of you not paying attention to what I just wrote, a "theolory" is the conflation of "theology" and "theory," hence "theolory." This chapter will supply the theoretical and theological foundations for an appreciation of humour. I have maintained that we normally operate with a bias against what the humorous perspective brings to the table, so I need to give a solid foundation or go home. Again, this is not to pit wit against a more sober-minded approach but to show how they complement each other.

A case in point: what follows are two short definitions of the same theological term "blasphemy." Note how the definitions are different but also how they complement each other.

> "Blasphemy: Irreverent and insulting or slanderous expressions against God."[1]

> "Blasphemy: If theology were butchery—and it often is—blasphemy would be the tools used to mar a sacred cow."[2]

Note how one matter-of-factly explains the term and the other playfully adds color and perspective. Most of us are not used to theological definitions with a pinch of spice, but for those of us who try to preach theology, it couldn't hurt. That's my point.

---

1. Erickson, *Concise Dictionary of Christian Theology*, 45/
2. Jacobson, *Crazy Talk*, 30

A "Theolory" of Wit

DEFINING WIT

I'll begin with the thankless task of trying to define humour, bearing in mind Robert Benchley's aphorism: "Defining and analyzing humour is a pastime of humorless people." The *Oxford English Dictionary* defines humour as "that quality of action, speech, or writing, which excites amusement, oddity, jocularity, facetiousness, comicality, fun."[3] While this definition is about as accurate as any, it's very much like dissecting a frog in high school biology class. By the time you have figured out how all the parts fit together, you have killed the frog. Nevertheless, we have a working definition and the majority of the time will be spent putting the proverbial meat on the bones (frogs legs anyone?).

THEORIES OF WIT

Humour theory is an interdisciplinary field much like many others, with a broad diversity of schools, theories, publications and luminaries. Among the various schools of thought, four main humour theories predominate: superiority, arousal, incongruity and reversal theories.

The superiority theories have the longest history, dating back as far as Plato (428–348 BC). They consider humour to be an expression of aggression whereby persons are amused by the misfortunes and/or imperfections of others. These theories are broad enough to incorporate the sense of "sudden glory rising" that comes from "getting the best" of difficult circumstances.[4] Aristotle's view of humour is representative of this constellation of theories:

> As for Comedy, it is . . . an imitation of men worse than average; worse, however, not as regards any or every sort of fault, but only as regards one particular kind, the Ridiculous, which is a species of the Ugly. The Ridiculous

---

3. *Oxford English Dictionary*, 2nd ed, s.v. "humour."
4. Martin, *The Psychology of Humor*, 44–49.

19

may be defined as a mistake or deformity not productive of pain or harm to others.[5]

Superiority theories emphasize the emotional and social aspects of humour and uncover the aggressive motivation in a lot of humour. These theories require the aid of incongruity theories in order to compensate for their deficiencies in explaining humour as a broad phenomenon.

Arousal theories of humour assume a complex mind-body interaction between cognition and emotion where the building of tension through various stimuli is relieved by its release in a socially acceptable manner. Humour is helpful in relieving the tension when it reaches an unpleasant level. Among the first to hold this view was Herbert Spencer (1820–1903 AD). The theorist to put this approach on the map was Sigmund Freud (1856–1939 AD) who recast the tension between cognition and emotion into the intra-psychic conflict between the id, ego and super ego. Humour became the means by which a person's sexual and aggressive impulses could outwit the censor (the super ego) and gain expression in some veiled form.[6] These theories tend to emphasize the biological and psychological aspects of humour and so are of greater interest to those who prefer experimentation over biblical exposition.

Incongruity theories ". . . suggest that the perception of incongruity is the crucial determinant of whether or not something is humorous: things that are funny are incongruous, surprising, peculiar, unusual, or different from what we normally expect."[7] Philosopher Immanuel Kant (1724–1804 AD) held to this theory of humour:

> Laughter is an affection arising from a strained expectation being suddenly reduced to nothing. This very reduction, at which certainly understanding cannot rejoice, is still indirectly a source of very likely enjoyment for a moment. Its cause must consequently be in the influence

---

5. Aristotle, *Poetics*, 1449 a 30.
6. Martin, *The Psychology of Humor*, 57–59.
7. Ibid., 63.

A "Theolory" of Wit

of the representation upon its body, and the reciprocal effect of this upon the mind.[8]

Arthur Koestler (1905–1983 AD), whom we met earlier, is a more recent proponent. His idea of bisociation occurs when "a situation, event, or idea is simultaneously perceived from the perspective of two self-consistent but normally incompatible or disparate frames of reference."[9] Incongruity theories emphasize the cognitive aspects of humour and tend to downplay the emotional and social aspects emphasized in the above theories.[10]

Reversal theories speak of the human capacity to revert to a more playful frame of mind on occasion (in contrast to a serious state of mind with its concerns for the future) and become open to the immediate appreciation of what appears to be playful or incongruous. Reversal theories tend to be composites of all the above theories. Rod Martin explains:

> ... the reversal theory perspective combines many of the elements of the other theories, emphasizing that humor is a form of play in which incongruities are enjoyed for their own sake in the context of our interactions with other people. It also highlights the diverse ways we experience humor,, including jokes, nonverbal humor, conversational witticisms, and the humorous outlook on the adversities of life that forms the basis for humor as a coping mechanism.[11]

For our purposes, the latter two groups of theories, the incongruity and reversal theories have the most explanatory power for the preacher's use of humour.

---

8. Kant, *The Critique of Judgment*, I 2.54.
9. Ibid.
10. Ibid., 74.
11. Ibid., 82.

With Wit and Wonder

A THEOLOGY OF WIT

Let's start with the one doing the theologizing. As in every activity, entering behavior helps establish how and where to begin the process. It also has a bearing on the trajectory of the theologizing. How should we begin a theological investigation of wit in Holy Writ? Theologian Thomas Oden suggests all theologians adopt what he calls "theo-comic perception":

> One who leaves no room for the utter unseriousness of theology will not be taken seriously in speaking of God.... The healthier the study of God, the more candid it remains about its finitude, the stubborn limits of its own knowing, its own charades, Band-Aids, closets, masks and broken windows. That is why the study of God is best understood within a caring community that laughs a little at its own somber efforts. Those whose faith offers corrective love empathetically to an atmosphere of theo-comic lightness about the pretended gravity of our words abounds.[12]

If Oden is right, we should have a head start here, since, hopefully, we have established the need to broaden our perception to include the kind of humility that comes from taking God seriously and everything else, especially ourselves, less so. Just so you do not suspect I am making all this up, I will be quoting generously from others sources so you can get a larger sense of who all is "in on this."

Wit's Cognate Terms

Oden states that theology is best undertaken within a caring community. Wit itself has its own family of associated terms which give us a broader appreciation for the matter at hand. A theology of wit is much more than a word study of the instances of "laughter" in the Bible. We need to understand at least two associated terms before we turn to the biblical texts themselves.

---

12. Oden, *The Living God*, 406.

A "Theolory" of Wit

Comedy.

Comedy is so much a part of our lives that it is difficult to describe with precision. At its root, comedy is a dramatic genre, composed of several sub-genres (e.g. romantic comedy, high comedy, low comedy, comedy of manners, and comedy of morals), designed primarily to amuse those in the audience. It is able to transcend its generic boundaries and has come to describe any work which deals with the limitations, foibles, failures and incongruities of the human condition and comes to a happy ending.[13] That is why works from ancient Greece, plays from Shakespeare's pen and the ubiquitous half hour sit coms (i.e. situation comedies) all have something in common. Everyone loves the down and out protagonist, who through a reversal of fortunes, ends up getting the girl, the dream job or whatever happens to be part of his wildest dreams.

So how does this relate at all to the Bible? More closely than you might imagine. The plot line of hopeless humanity experiencing a reversal of fortunes, gratuitously to boot, in order to be restored to everlasting paradise sounds a lot like the plot of redemptive history in Scripture. Literary critic Northrop Frye states the "the entire Bible, viewed as a "divine comedy" is contained within a U-shaped story of this sort, one in which man loses the tree and water of life at the beginning of Genesis and gets them back at the end of Revelation."[14] This basic idea of the U-shaped plot of the classic comedy has been developed into the figure of a check mark where the ending actually transcends the beginning, since in the biblical narrative Eden is eclipsed by heaven.[15]

Here is my attempt to capture the comedic form of the Bible's meta-narrative, which is entitled simply, The Story:

---

13. Holman and Harman, A *Handbook to Literature*, 95.
14. Frye, *The Great Code*, 167.
15. Edwards, "The World Could Not Contain the Books," 181.

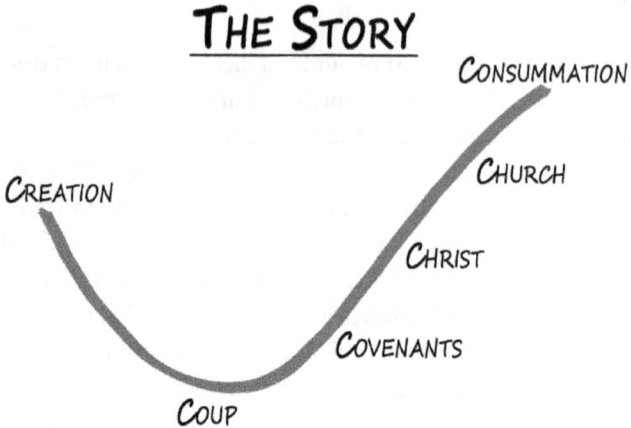

Each of the six plot points in the story might be summed up in one sentence. Creation: God creates everything. Coup: Humanity rebels against God. Covenants: God choses his own people as a light to all nations. Christ: God sends his own Son as our Savior. Church: Christ sends his body to make disciples. Consummation: God's plan of salvation will be complete.

If the biblical meta-narrative has this comedic shape to it, we might also suspect that some of the shorter narratives would take this same shape. We can see this in some biblical characters: Samson, Job, Jonah, Peter, the prodigal son of Luke 15 and even Jesus himself. This is not to say that comedic structure is the only interpretive structure in Scripture (e.g. Kings Saul and Solomon could hardly be called comedic characters but rather tragic ones), but it does suggest that a comedic reading of the Bible is not completely foreign to the overall message of redemption. This does give us a foothold at least in trying to trace the tracks of humour in Scripture.

Play.

A spirit of playfulness is closely related to a sense of humour. They feed off each other. Philosopher John Morreall suggests that "humour requires more than cleverness; it requires a playful attitude

A "Theolory" of Wit

toward what one is joking about."[16] Play is not just for children anymore. And since the term is used too widely now, we need to define exactly what we mean by it. We might say that we play a sport but then expend more energy there than what we do at work. There are also professional athletes who say they are "players" (i.e. football players, hockey players, etc.), but can you truly play a game when you are paid handsomely and expected to perform admirably?

True play is characterized by six attributes:

1. Play requires that all assumptions are provisional and conditional because in play make-believe becomes real.
2. Play requires a form of reference and parameters or "rules" which may be changed in systematic ways.
3. Play requires that phenomenal forms (toys) can be transformed through the imagination but this transformation is constrained to some degree by the original forms themselves (i.e. there is only so far that imagination can take you)
4. Play brings into being something that has not existed before by changing the shape and positioning of parts of the game.
5. Play requires a changeable medium that mirrors the qualities of creativity and imagination.
6. Play calls for the questioning of any forms or rules that claim to be the truth.[17]

Theologians have tried to interpret play theologically. Back in the 1960s and 1970s, when everything else seemed up for grabs, several theologians were working hard on theologies of play. Some were captured by the spirit of the times and were looking for new ways to kick down the traces, but others were trying to explore this phenomenon and give it direction and limitations. "Players" in this field included Jürgen Moltmann, Georg Gadamer, Harvey Cox, David Miller, Hugo Rahner, Johan Huizinga, and evangelical Robert Johnston. Time pressed on and this body of work seemed to fade along with Woodstock and Beatle haircuts, but remnants of a

16. Morreall, *Taking Laughter Seriously*, 136.
17. Handleman, "Play," n/p.

playful theological perspective remain. David Miller states it best: "It is therefore not enough for a *theological ludens* [theology of play] to be a theology about play, interpreting traditional doctrines of the faith. . . . It must not only be *about* play; it must also be a theology *of* play, *by* play, and *for* play. It must wittingly incarnate its content."[18]

So in what way does play fit in with how humour and comedy relate to theology? Theologian Conrad Hyers explains:

> The essential element in relation to the sacred is the periodic suspension of seriousness and sacrality (the comic spirit) and the realization of the playful, game-like quality inherent in all human enterprises, however holy (the comic perspective). The spirit of comedy is kindled by that same spirit of play that lies within the very nature of things themselves, from atoms to 'little creeping things' to whirling galaxies to homo sapiens, who nervously tries to comprehend the whole in neat little packages of rationality, order, and meaning—the element of indeterminacy and randomness, of vitality and spontaneity, yes, or purposeless being and becoming for the sake of being and becoming.[19]

It becomes more obvious that humour, comedy and play are intertwined in giving us a different perspective from which we can explore the Scriptures. Again, this is not to say we will never use another perspective, but at least our eyesight has been broadened to look for what we might not have noticed before.

By this time, I'm not sure whether you are expecting much more from a theology of humour or much less. Your chances of the latter are far greater. I will not attempt to echo traditional doctrines from a humorous perspective (if that is your interest, I suggest you read *Crazy Talk: A Not-So-Stuffy Dictionary of Theological Terms* edited by Rolf A. Jacobson or *A Comedian's Guide to Theology* by Thor Ramsey). All I will attempt here is to highlight a few theological themes which will complement traditional theologies but also undergird the employment of a more humorous or playful perspective in reading biblical texts when that is warranted. What you will

18. Miller, *Gods and Games*, 259.
19. Hyers, *Holy Laughter*, 7.

notice immediately is how fragmentary and incomplete it is, but again I remind you, I'm only playing!

Theology Proper (or Improper)

Real theologies begin with God. This is where I'll start too—not with a complex discussion of the Trinity or a catalogue of divine attributes, but one simple suggestion. There isn't much more I can say, especially since I need to leave a discussion of the doctrine of creation until the next chapter. All I would want to say at this time is that God is beautiful. Traditional theologies often have an impressive list of divine attributes and I would whole-heartedly agree with all of that. I just notice that relatively few theologians highlight God's beauty. I think we should take pains to ponder God's beauty because that will help us appreciate him in a way that passes beyond mere cognitive acknowledgement. I keep hearing a faint echo in my head of a line from Tim Keller: "Religious people find God useful; Christians find God beautiful." Now that's great theology! Should we not bask in God's glorious beauty? Not in some abstract way that realizes God has this quality in his being, but that he *is* beautiful and we encounter him *as* beautiful. Should that not elicit joyful and obedient worship? Should that not open our eyes to realities that stretch beyond our capacities to communicate?

I offer the words of one theologian, Karl Barth (who seldom forgets to write about anything), as he sees God's beauty as part of his glory:

> It is to say that God has this superior force, this power of attraction, which speaks for itself, which wins and conquers, on the fact that he is beautiful, divinely beautiful, beautifully in His own way, in a way that is His alone, beautiful as the unattainable primal beauty, yet really beautiful. He does not have it, therefore merely as a fact or a power. Or rather, He has it as a fact and a power in such a way that He acts as the One who gives pleasure, creates desire and rewards with enjoyment. And He does it because He is pleasant, desirable, full of enjoyment, because first and last He alone is that which is pleasant,

desirable and full of enjoyment. God loves us as the One who is worthy of love as God. This is what we mean when we say that God is beautiful.[20]

Barth is never caught for words and so goes on to give three illustrations of God's beauty: his unity, the Trinity and the Incarnation.[21] This beauty invokes our response—joy: "Joy in and before God—in its particular nature, distinct from what we mean by awe, gratitude and the rest—has an objective basis. It is something in God, the God of all perfections, which justifies us in having joy, desire and pleasure towards Him, which indeed obliges, summons and attracts us to do this."[22] Joy is just around the block from laughter and humour, so all these responses can join in on the celebration.

The Quest for the Hysterical Jesus

There is nothing I could add to the person and work of Christ that we can't find in much better form in traditional theologies. The one thing we usually cannot find is biblical evidence that Jesus used humorous devices in his preaching and teaching. Here is where I will spend my time. However, investigating Jesus' use of humour opens a Pandora's box of questions. Some feel it is hard to speak of Jesus's humour without button-holing him into some kind of first century sectarian identity. So it is important to say from the outset what I am not saying about Jesus' humour and what I am saying.

What I'm not saying: I am not trying to place Jesus as a member of some particular political, religious or philosophical group in his day. My goal is simply to understand the humorous devices Jesus uses. The first task, then, is to clear the brush away of all the speculative theories that paint Jesus with a particular religious or philosophical stripe.

Harvey Cox suggested in the turbulence of the 1960s that Jesus could be viewed as a harlequin or jester figure due to the similarities he saw between Jesus and the usual countercultural

20. Barth, *The Doctrine of God*, 650, 651.
21. Ibid., 657–66.
22. Ibid., 655.

A "Theolory" of Wit

lampooning that was part of the clown's *modus operandi*.[23] Cox had no alternative textual basis for his views but seemed to put the canonical picture of Jesus through the lens of the anti-establishment sentiments of that era.

Jesus has also been pictured in the form of the trickster—the unscrupulous preternatural practical joker found in the mythologies of several traditions, including classical, Scandinavian and North American Aboriginal religions. Donald Blais has suggested that several of Jesus' actions and words could be related to the basic characteristics of the trickster—his sharing of human and divine dimensions, his flouting of cultural mores, his mastery over demons, his abilities to change form and avoid capture as well as his fondness for playful interchange.[24] While there may be some commonalities, Jesus never shares the capricious attitude of the garden-variety trickster.

While the above approaches assume a certain slant on the canonical gospels, there are versions of Jesus based upon differing textual bases. Gnostic texts have a rather different picture of Jesus—one who employs his divine powers for selfish and childish ends and who laughs at his own crucifixion since the Romans actually crucified another.[25] This portrait of Jesus with the capricious nature of his actions, the derisiveness of his laughter and the denial of his humanity is obviously inferior to the picture of Jesus painted in the canonical gospels.

Other views of Jesus are built upon revisionist views of history. Tom Harpur has reconstructed a view of Jesus that depends upon parallels with selected ancient Egyptian traditions that were promoted by obscure Egyptologist Alvin Kuhn (1880–1963).[26] Besides being severely criticized for its methodology, Harpur's view of Jesus is so highly spiritualized that any discussion of what this Jesus might have said, humorous or otherwise, seems to beg the question.

23. Cox, *Feast of Fools*, 140, 141.

24. Blais, "Jesus the Christ," 5–8.

25. Irenaeus, *Against the Heresies*, I.24.4; Elliot, *The Apocryphal New Testament*, 76.

26. Harpur, *The Pagan Christ*.

With Wit and Wonder

Views of Jesus as an itinerant Cynic sage have received increasing attention in the past three decades. Cynics were famous for their criticism of self-indulgent societal structures and lives spent chasing self-gratification. Their mastery of the *chreia* or aphorism (or memorable one-liners, if you like) make the connection between Jesus as a Cynic and his use of humour a tempting one. Several versions of the Cynic thesis exist[27] but they are all based on somewhat speculative historical reconstructions and employ some stretching of the sources and display circular reasoning.[28]

What I am saying: it should be obvious that we don't have to fit Jesus into a particular mold in order to understand his use of humour. I believe Jesus was influenced much more by the various canonical and rabbinical traditions that came from within his own Jewish heritage. It is here that we find interesting insights into Jesus' humour.

The Hebrew prophetic tradition is not exactly famous for eliciting laughter but a close reading of the canonical texts suggests that on occasion the prophets used humorous devices to their advantage. Given the role of social critic, most prophetic humour was more of a polemic nature with irony and satire predominating. Elijah's baiting the prophets of Baal on Mount Carmel (1 Kings 18:16-46) and Isaiah's polemic against idols (44:9-20) are obvious examples of prophetic humour.[29]

Another formative influence might be the Hebrew wisdom tradition. If we recognize two basic streams of wisdom thought, the more conventional proverbial type and the more subversive, speculative variety, we might expect differing uses and forms of humour to be present. Proverbial wisdom, primarily delivered in aphoristic forms (the "proverbial" one-liner) is better suited to the obvious uses of caricature, parody, hyperbole and absurdity. For example, Proverbs 11:22: "Like a gold ring in a pig's snout is a beautiful woman without discretion." Since Jesus did not produce

---

27. Downing, *Cynics and Christian Origins*; Vaage, *Galilean Upstarts*; Borg, *Jesus: A New Vision*.

28. Wright, *Jesus and the Victory of God*, 83-124.

29. Carroll, "Is Humour Also Among the Prophets?" 169-89; cf. Good, *Irony in the Old Testament*.

A "Theolory" of Wit

any written documents, the more subtle humorous devices found in The Writings would not serve his purposes as readily as the proverbial forms.[30]

The rabbinical tradition both precedes and succeeds the time of Jesus; therefore a wholesale importing of this rich heritage as a formative influence for Jesus' humour would be anachronistic at best. And similar to the other influences discussed above, our point is not to support the primacy of humour in them or even the necessity of Jesus imbibing his humour from them, but to establish the possibility that they serve as a backdrop for Jesus' wit.

In his monograph *Humour and Irony in the New Testament Illustrated by Parallels in Talmud and Midrash*, Jacob Jonsson notes:

> The rabbinic literature does not reveal a melancholic or pessimistic attitude towards life. On the contrary it seems to be inspired with a certain kind of joy and happiness. The playful mind is able to find something amusing and humorous, even when dealing with the most serious matters. I think that this inspiration is due to the fact that the rabbinical students and scholars always had it impressed upon their minds that Torah itself was a gift from God who cares for his people, and it should be studied with joy and gladness.... The humour of the old Hebrews was a religious and serious kind of humour, and it is sometimes difficult to decide whether a talmudic passage actually is serious or humorous, because it is both at the same time.[31]

A possible example of the melding of the serious with the humorous is the rabbinical saying: "Who is a man of piety that is a fool? He, for example, who, if a woman is drowning, says, 'It is unseemly for me look at her, and therefore I cannot rescue her.'"[32]

---

30. Whedbee, *The Bible and the Comic Vision*, 129–90; 221–77. Cf. Radday and Brenner, *On Humour*, 217–313.
31. Jonsson, *Humor and Irony in the New Testament*, 89.
32. Montifiore and Loewe, *A Rabbinic Anthology*, 487.

With Wit and Wonder

Examples of Jesus' Humour.

What remains is to give at least a sampling of the humorous devices Jesus used.

SATIRE

Satire is a work or manner that blends a censorious attitude with humour and wit for the sake of improving some human behaviour or institution. Satirists attempt by the use of laughter not simply to tear down but to inspire a remodeling since they are often personally involved with the objects of their criticism. A good satirist is responsible enough to realize that their proposed remedy must not be seen by the audience as more repulsive than the disease. Many different devices may have a satirical intent. Jesus' contrast of John the Baptist with the pampered royal courtiers serves as a case in point:

> When John's messengers had gone, Jesus began to speak to the crowds concerning John: "What did you go out into the wilderness to see? A reed shaken by the wind? What then did you go out to see? A man dressed in soft clothing? Behold, those who are dressed in splendid clothing and live in luxury are in kings' courts. What then did you go out to see? A prophet? Yes, I tell you, and more than a prophet. This is he of whom it is written,
>
> "'Behold, I send my messenger before your face, who will prepare your way before you.'
>
> I tell you, among those born of women none is greater than John. Yet the one who is least in the kingdom of God is greater than he." Luke 7:24-28

IRONY

Verbal irony "is a statement in which the meaning that the speaker implies differs sharply from the meaning that is ostensibly expressed."³³ Jesus' cryptic response to the report of Herod's death threat displays ironic qualities:

> And he said to them, "Go and tell that fox, 'Behold, I cast out demons and perform cures today and tomorrow, and the third day I finish my course. Nevertheless, I must go on my way today and tomorrow and the day following, *for it cannot be that a prophet should perish away from Jerusalem*' (not the usual way Jews viewed Jerusalem!). Luke 13:32, 33

Dramatic irony "involves a situation in a play or a narrative in which the audience or reader shares with the author knowledge of present or future circumstances of which a character is ignorant. . . ."³⁴ The retort of Cleopas to the resurrected Jesus on the road to Emmaus, "Are you the only visitor in Jerusalem who does not know the things that have happened there in these days?" (Luke 24:18b), drips with dramatic irony.

Invective/Ridicule

Invective is defined as "the denunciation of a person by the use of derogatory epithets."³⁵ Northrop Frye somewhat rehabilitates the potential mean-spiritedness of the attack by stating that "invective is never the expression of merely personal hatred, whatever the motivation for it may be . . . For effective attack we must reach some kind of impersonal level, and that commits the attacker . . . to a moral standard."³⁶ The collection of "woe statements" in Matthew 23:13–32 is an example of invective.

> "Woe to you, scribes and Pharisees, hypocrites! For you are like whitewashed tombs, which outwardly appear beautiful, but within are full of dead people's bones and all uncleanness. So you also outwardly appear righteous

---

33. Abrams, *A Glossary of Literary Terms*, 135.
34. Ibid., 136, 137.
35. Ibid., 134.
36. Frye, "The Nature of Satire," 18, 19.

> to others, but within you are full of hypocrisy and lawlessness. Matt 23:27, 28.

So much for "Jesus, meek and mild!"

Sarcasm

Sarcasm (literally, "flesh-tearing") refers to "the crude and taunting use of apparent praise for dispraise."[37] It does soften the direct personal attack in contrast to invective by employing inversion to make the impact more indirect. Jesus was using sarcasm when he said to the Pharisees, ". . . Those who are well have no need of a physician, but those who are sick. Go and learn what this means: 'I desire mercy, and not sacrifice.' For I came to call not the righteous but sinners" (Matt 9:12, 13).

Burlesque

The essence of burlesque is a discrepancy between subject matter and style.[38] Parody (high burlesque) is when a weighty style is used in relation to relatively inconsequential subject matter. Jesus uses parody when he criticizes the religious leaders:

> He answered them, "When it is evening, you say, 'It will be fair weather, for the sky is red.' And in the morning, 'It will be stormy today, for the sky is red and threatening.' You know how to interpret the appearance of the sky, but you cannot interpret the signs of the times. Matt 16:2, 3.

Travesty (low burlesque) is when a weighty subject is addressed in lesser style.

> "To what then shall I compare the people of this generation, and what are they like? They are like children sitting in the marketplace and calling to one another,
> "'We played the flute for you, and you did not dance; we sang a dirge, and you did not weep.'

---

37. Abrams, *A Glossary of Literary Terms*, 136.
38. Ibid., 26–28.

A "Theolory" of Wit

> For John the Baptist has come eating no bread and drinking no wine, and you say, 'He has a demon.' The Son of Man has come eating and drinking, and you say, 'Look at him! A glutton and a drunkard, a friend of tax collectors and sinners!' Luke 7:31–34.

Caricature is when the qualities of a person are exaggerated to produce a ridiculous effect. Caricature and invective are combined when Jesus rails, "Woe to you, scribes and Pharisees, hypocrites! For you travel across sea and land to make a single proselyte, and when he becomes a proselyte, you make him twice as much a child of hell as yourselves" (Matt 23:15).

All of these examples display Jesus' use of humorous devices. There also are other broader figures of speech which Jesus uses humorously.

Hyperbole

Hyperbole (literally, "over-shooting") is "bold overstatement, or the extravagant exaggeration of fact or of possibility. It may be used either for serious or ironic or comic effect."[39] Jesus was rather fond of hyperbole: "Why do you see the speck that is in your brother's eye, but do not notice the log that is in your own eye?" (Matt 7:3); "It is easier for a camel to go through the eye of a needle than for a rich person to enter the kingdom of God" (Mark 10:25); "You blind guides, straining out a gnat and swallowing a camel!" (Matt 23:24).

Meiosis

Meiosis, in contrast to the overstatement of hyperbole, "deliberately represents something as very much less in magnitude or importance than it really is, or is ordinarily considered to be."[40] Jesus combines meiosis with a rhetorical question when he asks, "Does he thank the servant because he did what was commanded" (which

---

39. Ibid., 120.
40. Ibid.

would elicit a "You're not kidding!" from those familiar with the institution of slavery in those days)? (Luke 17:9).

Riddle

Riddles are verbal puzzles which not only display the verbal and intellectual ingenuity and playfulness of the one who poses them but also requires the same of those who would be able to answer them. Jesus' statement in John 2:19, "... Destroy this temple, and in three days I will raise it up" is in the form of a riddle.[41] Mark records two of Jesus' riddles in the same chapter: "There is nothing outside a person that by going into him can defile him, but the things that come out of a person are what defile him" (7:15); "Let the children be fed first, for it is not right to take the children's bread and throw it to the dogs" (7:27).

Paradox

Paradox is defined as "a statement which seems on its face to be logically contradictory or absurd, yet turns out to be interpretable in a way that makes good sense."[42] Paradox is well-suited to the expression of arresting truths. Jesus' preaching of 'the kingdom of God' (the unifying theme of his teaching) depended a great deal on the provocative power of statements like: "Leave the dead to bury their own dead. But as for you, go and proclaim the kingdom of God" (Luke 9:60); "For to the one who has, more will be given, and from the one who has not, even what he has will be taken away" (Mark 4:25); "For whoever would save his life will lose it, but whoever loses his life for my sake and the gospel's, will save it" (Mark 8:35); "If anyone would be firs, het must be last of all and servant of all" (Mark 9:35b); "But many who are first will be last, and the last first" (Mark 10:31); "Truly I say to you, unless you turn and become like children, you will never enter the kingdom of heaven. Whoever humbles himself like this child is the greatest in the

---

41. Beasley-Murray, *Jesus and the Kingdom of God*, 41.
42. Abrams, *A Glossary of Literary Terms*, 201.

kingdom of heaven" (Matt 18:3, 4); and "Whoever exalts himself will be humbled, and whoever humbles himself will be exalted" (Matt 23:12). These paradoxical statements show both the playful and subversive nature of the kingdom of God. Philosopher Simon Critchley notes, "From the standpoint of the worldly-wise, Christ appears to be a kind of madman. Where the world admires money, power and success, the Christian indifference to these values turns the secular world upside down . . . Christianity offers us a topsy-turvy world that inverts our worldly values."[43]

Here is where our search for the hysterical Jesus ends. It's enough to realize Jesus' humour was contextually relevant and served the greater ends of the Kingdom of God. Since he has modeled how to suffer (1 Pet 2:21), we also can take our cues from him in how we use our own wit. In this way, as in all others, Jesus is both our Model and our Messiah.

Oh, the Humanity!

Theological anthropology gives us a biblical picture of both the height of our status (created in God's image) and the depths of our sinfulness. The humorous perspective has something to contribute to both of these doctrines.

In God's Image.

Humanity is the apex of creation, the crowning achievement of God's creative work.

> Then God said, "Let us make man in our image, after our likeness. And let them have dominion over the fish of the sea and over the birds of the heavens, and over the livestock and over all the earth, and over every creeping thing that creeps on the earth." So God created man in His own image, in the image of God he created him; male and female he created them (Gen 1:26, 27).

---

43. Critchley, *On Humour*, 16.

While views of this image vary greatly among theologies,[44] there is an agreement that it forms the qualitative difference between humanity and the rest of creation. As a result of this special gift, humanity is singled out for special honor. Barth described this honor as ". . . the significance, the worth, the distinction, which he [humanity] now has in the eyes of God; the value, which is now ascribed to him by the mouth and in the word of God; the adornment, vesture and crown with which he is now clothed by God."[45]

This bestowed honor is manifest in a number of ways. One way in which humanity reflects the divine imprimatur, according to sociologist Peter Berger, is through signals of transcendence. Human tendencies such as: order, play, hope and damnation, along with humour, give unique witness to the existence of God.[46] The ability for self-transcendence places humanity above the rest of creation and an ability to view reality from a humorous perspective is an essential part of this divine gift.

Humour is not only seen as an expression of the divine image but also as an appropriate human response to it. Barth outlines that pure thankfulness, deepest humility and free humour are the necessary human postures in relation to the honor bestowed by God. In relation to the last, he remarks, "humour is the opposite of all self-admiration and praise. The honor of man comes from the God who is alone to be admired and praised. How can it be recognized, affirmed, and seized except in the free humour which takes and keeps its distance?"[47] Barth himself is a good example of this sane self-estimation in the light of God's endowments. In light-hearted fashion he remarks about his theological efforts:

> The angels laugh at old Karl. They laugh at him because he tries to grasp the truth about God in a book of Dogmatics. They laugh at the fact that volume follows volume and each is thicker than the previous one. As they laugh,

---

44. Grenz, *Theology for the Community of God*, 218–33.
45. Barth, *The Doctrine of Creation*, III.4, 663.
46. Berger, *A Rumour of Angels*, 86–90.
47. Barth, *The Doctrine of Creation*, III.4, 665.

A "Theolory" of Wit

they say to one another, "Look! Here he comes now with his little pushcart full of volumes of the *Dogmatics*!"[48]

From this brief discussion, humour appears not to be a frivolous option for those so included, but an integral part of being human and a necessary part of responding to the human condition.

Born to Lose.

The other side of this coin is the depth of human sinfulness. To charge that the humorous perspective does not take sin seriously is to misunderstand the situation. If humour is that quality which highlights the distinction between the infinite and the finite, it not only takes sin seriously but can interpret sin as seriousness—the idolatrous self-preoccupation of humans who take themselves too seriously. Such a realization gives a new perspective on the fall of humanity and human sinfulness.

> The fall is, if anything, the loss of laughter, not the loss of seriousness. Adam and Eve fell when they began to take themselves, their "deprivations," and their ambitions too seriously. And we have taken ourselves, our opinions and beliefs, our status and achievements, and our designs on the universe too seriously ever since.[49]

The humorous perspective engages sin and evil seriously in that it refuses to accept them as the final word in a world created by a holy and redeeming God. In other words, sin is taken seriously by not taking it too seriously. Sin and evil are viewed with realistic fear and suspicion and are exposed and opposed by a sense of prophetic humour among other responses.

This is not to say, of course, that the laughter of humans themselves may not be affected by sinfulness. Conrad Hyers has suggested at least three levels of humour. The first is the laughter of "paradise." This form of humour is innocent and childlike where one indulges in a harmless bit of silliness or absurdity. Elephant

---

48. Barth, *Portrait of Karl Barth*, 3.
49. Hyers, *And God Created Laughter*, 14.

jokes belong to this category of pure playfulness. The laughter of "paradise lost" is where innocence is lost, and one must live with the tensions inherent within reality. This kind of humour may express itself in lower forms of base humour where it serves to be a vicious weapon. It may also be seen in higher forms as prophetic humour which aims to pop the bubble of human pretension and aids in catharsis. The final level is the laughter of "paradise regained." It is the humour among close friends based upon grace, caring and trust. It is laughing "with" rather than laughing "at."[50] So, when we contemplate who we are as humans—created in God's image, yet fallen but redeemable by God's grace—we are more than just *homo sapiens* (wise or thinking man), we are also *homo ludens* (playing man) and *homo ridens* (laughing man).

Virtuous Reality.

The Bible contains several different lists of virtues for Christians to practice. We need to practice them because we often get them wrong! While I will hardly do justice to the doctrine of the Christian life by noting three of its chief virtues (i.e. faith, love and gratitude), it is a start and you might see enough to take it from there.

Funny Faith.

Can we be both faithful and funny at the same time? How are they related? Theologian Reinhold Niebuhr found a connection between them but also wanted to prioritize faith over humour when push comes to shove. He notes, "The intimate relation between humour and faith is derived from the fact that both deal with the incongruities of our existence. Humour is concerned with the immediate incongruities of life and faith with the ultimate ones."[51] He may have underestimated the degree of interpenetration between these two concepts. When one addresses a matter of ultimate incongruity, can it truly be said that the necessary faith lacks any sense of

50. Hyers, *The Comic Vision and the Christian Faith*, 32–39.
51. Niebuhr, "Humour and Faith," 135.

the humorous? Does faith debar any recognition of the tenuousness of the human condition in the course of addressing even the most threatening issues? Niebuhr's fear is that employing humour by itself to deal with ultimate issues will lead to meaninglessness and to that extent he is correct. Where he is mistaken is in missing the closeness of the relationship between humour and faith. There are countless examples where people have used to humour to cope with even the most horrendous situations—hence the term "gallows humour." The symbiotic relationship between faith and humour is better understood by agreeing with Hyers, "The relationship between faith and humor is an intimate one. On the one side is the peril of idolatry and pride. On the other side is the peril of unbelief and despair. Faith without humor becomes fanaticism; humor without faith becomes cynicism."[52]

Crazy Love.

Sharing life and love with each other inevitably means sharing laughter. Sharing humour together indicates an intimacy and empathy that should make believers stand out from the crowd. Part of life in Christ is being able to rejoice with those who rejoice (Romans 12:15). Now might be the right time for the entry for "love" in *Crazy Talk: A Not-So-Stuffy Dictionary of Theological Terms*:

> You can't love your car. Or your house. Or your rubber ducky. Your car/house/ducky may be nicer than any of ours, but if you "love" them, you're really just loving what you have—thus, you are just being devoted to your own self, your own pleasure, and your own happiness. If you think you can love your car, you need a whack upside the head and a serious reevaluation of priorities.
>
> Love is not a sentiment or an emotion. It is not something you feel but action you take on behalf of others. And love certainly isn't blind. Love stares the suffering and needs of the neighbor—and even of the enemy!—hard in the face. And then does something about them.

---

52. Hyers, *And God Created Laughter*, 27.

If you have a problem with this, you might have a problem with God. We are only able to love because God first loved us (1 John 3:16). God's very nature is love, since God's actions of creation, redemption, and sanctification are continuous acts of love. Seeing as the world doesn't stop existing for people who are jerks, we can know that God's love is unconditional.[53]

The Grateful Living.

Gratitude is an appropriate response to the gift of salvation. In the words of Karl Barth, ". . .gratitude means specifically that I am gladly, i.e. voluntarily and cheerfully, ready for what God wills of me in acknowledgement of what is given to me by God and as my necessary response to God's gift."[54] Barth's argument is complex, determining gratitude to be an eschatological and free response, but it is his understanding of the expression of gratitude that is of interest here. Gratitude is to be expressed in play:

> At this point, where we understand the required character of our action to be gratitude, it is in place to consider the bold thesis that our conduct bears the mark of good, of what is pleasing to God, when it is not done in earnest but in play. . . .Having said this, we should not fail to say that as God's children we are in fact released from the seriousness of life and can and should simply play before God.[55]

Playful gratitude, according to Barth, is expressed in art and humour, and his view of humour is hardly cavalier but rather rooted in the eschaton (Personal confession: if you are wondering about the number of quotations from Barth, I need to confess that I spend time each week in the morning of my day off with a group of students, faculty and pastors to discuss our recent reading of the *Church Dogmatics*. I know that doesn't sound either funny or

53. Jacobson, *Crazy Talk*, 110.
54. Barth, *Ethics*, 499, 500.
55. Ibid., 503, 504.

A "Theolory" of Wit

creative, so that is why you won't find this fact on the book jacket. But just in case you were wondering, Barth does have a theology of humour: humour is the freedom to laugh at ourselves, assumes rather than excludes the reality of suffering, and is grounded on God's grace, faithfulness and beauty[56]):

> ... humour undoubtedly means that we do not take the present with ultimate seriousness, not because it is not serious enough in itself, but because God's future, which breaks into the present, is more serious. Humour means the placing of a big bracket around the seriousness of the present. In no way does it mean—and those who think it does do not know what real humour is—that this seriousness is set aside or dismissed. Humour arises, and can arise only, when we wrestle with this seriousness of the present. But above and in this wrestling, we cannot be totally serious as the children of God.[57]

The End is Near.

Speaking of the end of time, my last doctrine, appropriately enough, is eschatology. I will not be giving a humorous version of an end times chart (because most of these are funny enough on their own) or highlighting the battle of the millennial theories. I will simply draw your attention to hope.

Whispering Hope.

Both hope and humour recognize the eschatological tension between the "already" and the "not yet." The present time, between the inauguration and consummation of the age to come, is full of all the incongruities one might expect for believers whose citizenship is in heaven (Phil 3:20) while they continue to live as inhabitants of the earth. Humour helps believers to cope with the many difficult situations of life by daring to believe in hope—in something more

---

56. Migliore, *"Karl Barth: Theologian with a Sense of Humor,"* 277, 278.
57. Barth, *Ethics*, 511.

43

than the present evidence of hopelessness. By responding to the incongruities of present existence in good humour, believers display Christian hope. In the words of Harvey Cox, "Only by assuming a playful attitude toward our religious tradition can we possibly make any sense of it. Only by learning to laugh at the hopelessness around us can we touch the hem of hope."[58] The ability to face life's incongruities is not a baseless hope or a hope against hope. True hope is based on a commitment to the plans and purposes of God to bring about his will in human history. Hope and humour recognize the present in light of the future and so their response to the present and their faith in the future honor the God who will bring his purposes to pass. Hope and humour become part of the interim ethic to guide believers until the end. Frederick Buechner sums up this basis trust in God's purposes by saying, "Where there is humor, there is hope; where there is hope, there is humor. The tragic is the inevitable; the comic is the unforeseeable."[59] We can see humour, then, as our stepping into the eschatological promise of Jesus' blessing, "Blessed are you who weep now, for you shall laugh" (Luke 6:21b).

Really all I am arguing for is a truly gospel-inspired understanding of humour. Tim Keller explains it well:

> Moralism eats away at real joy and humor because the system of legalism forces us to take our self (our image, our appearance, our reputation) *very* seriously. Relativism/pragmatism on the other hand, tends toward pessimism as life goes on because of the inevitable cynicism that grows from lack of hope for the world ("In the end, evil will triumph because there is no judgment or divine justice"). If we are saved by grace alone, this salvation is a constant source of amazed delight. Nothing is mundane or matter-of-fact about our lives. It is a miracle we are Christians, and the gospel, which creates bold humility, should give us a far deeper sense of humor and joy. We

---

58. Cox, *Feast of Fools*, 156, 157.
59. Buechner, *Telling the Truth*, 57.

A "Theolory" of Wit

don't have to take ourselves seriously, and we are full of hope for the world.[60]

So there you have it, the "theolory" of wit. You now have at least some idea of the definition, the theories and a theology of humour. Now we're going to turn around and do this all over again for wonder (imagination). Are we having fun yet?

---

60. Keller, *Center Church*, 50, 51.

2 | A "Theolory" of Wonder

So now we turn our attention to wonder—that capacity that helps us see through and around and between what is seen to what is unseen. This requires something other than a fancy pair of X-ray glasses, some altered state of consciousness, or some chemically-induced high—in case you are still worried that this right-brained stuff is a bit sketchy. I will basically retrace my steps from the last chapter, but this time in relation to wonder rather than wit. In many ways, since wit and wonder are cousins, this chapter and the previous one cover some of the same territory since much of what can be said of wit can also be said of wonder. The result is that this chapter will assume much of the same theological grounding and therefore, mercifully, will be shorter.

DEFINING WONDER

As prosaic as it may sound, we should start with the task of defining wonder. We immediately run into a small issue, since there are two terms used to describe what I am talking about: imagination and creativity. Technically, these terms have separate meanings and histories, but in contemporary usage, they are practically interchangeable. It is hard to know which one to choose, so I chose neither and went with "wonder" (partly to reduce the confusion and partly due to the fact that "wonder" alliterates nicely with "wit"!).

A "Theolory" of Wonder

There are many competing definitions for both imagination and creativity and so rather than listing them all, or having to choose between then, I am opting to go with the definitions found in the *Oxford English Dictionary* like I did with "humour." It seemed like such a waste to trash the many other definitions that surfaced, so I have placed some of them in Appendix B for your information and inspiration.

> Imagination: the faculty or action of forming new ideas, or images or concepts of external objects not present to the senses.[1]
>
> Creativity: the use of imagination or original ideas to create something; inventiveness.[2]

Although there is some affinity between these two, we might say that imagination is a way of *perceiving* and creativity is a way of *conceiving*. The two tend to interpenetrate because often our conceiving is the result of our perceiving. In what follows, I will usually refer to "imagination" and "creativity" as virtual synonyms and will assume they can both be subsumed under the umbrella term "wonder." So then let me suggest the following about "wonder": wonder is the capacity to shape or order a new form of reality by perceiving new qualities in things and discovering previously unseen relationships between things. It is the creative interplay between discipline and freedom, convention and innovation, time and timeliness, work and playfulness (creation and re-creation). Maybe I should have stayed with the dictionary definitions!

THEORIES OF WONDER

The world of wonder is complex because preachers are not the only ones out there who want a piece of this pie. Educators, neurobiologists, philosophers, psychologists, sociologists, economists, scientists and business persons are all lining up for their share. Many of the competing theories betray the assumptions of those promoting

1. *Oxford English Dictionary*, 2nd ed, s.v. "imagination."
2. *Oxford English Dictionary*, 2nd ed, s.v. "creativity."

them. Nothing new there, just that it does make summarizing the main competitors a daunting task. To help, I'll be looking mainly at what might be termed more metaphorical or subjective theories rather than the more traditionally objective or scientific ones. While the latter often play some part in the former, to be preoccupied with matters of empirical verifiability often, ironically, limits the possibility of "hard" science to measure what is mostly intuitive in practice. The same criticism of the humorless studying humour might be leveled against those inside-the-box types who study that which is outside the box. Another emphasis I'll employ is to focus more on the everyday expressions of creativity (referred to often as "little-c") rather the more exceptional accomplishments of the creative giants and geniuses (often termed "BIG-C"). I'm assuming the majority of you fall into the former category with me because those who are true creative geniuses have long since put this book down (in at least two ways!). With these preferences in place, the best way to navigate this diverse landscape is to describe the dominant factors in the study of wonder under the headings of: process, product, person and place.[3]

Process.

Theories that fall under this heading "aim to understand the nature of the mental mechanisms that occur when a person is engaged in creative thinking or creative activity."[4] These theories focus on how creative thought takes place and how creative products are produced. Some of these theories explore the actual thought processes by which problems are identified and solved creatively and wonder becomes reality.[5]

One of these theories would be the honing theory developed by Liane Gabora. Honing theory highlights the role of a person's worldview in the creative process. We all have an understanding of the world which serves as a filter for how we deal with anomalies

---

3. Kozbelt, et al., "Theories of Creativity," 24.
4. Ibid.
5. Ibid., 33–35.

or challenges to that world view. We attempt to understand the unknown by connecting it to what we already know to be true. These connections may stretch our current worldview in some way as they point out inadequacies in our older understanding. So some of these connections not only influence the results of our inquiry, but can also influence or hone our worldview as well. The point is, our worldviews do not tend to be written in stone and so should adjust to the new reality when our creative processes take us beyond these old understandings. A creative person's product comes from this process which reflects his/her unique view of the world. This helps to explain a person's creative style and why some creative people seem to live in a world different than the one we woke up in this morning.[6]

The theories that seem most pertinent for our purposes under this category are the stage and componential process theories which, as you might expect, focus on the various stages within the creative process. The most enduring of these theories was developed by Graham Wallas, who divided the creative thinking process into four stages.

> The first in time I shall call Preparation, the stage during which the problem was "investigated . . . in all directions"; the second stage during which he was not consciously thinking about the problem, which I shall call Incubation; the third, consisting of the appearance of the "happy idea" together with the psychological events which immediately preceded and accompanied that appearance, I shall call Illumination. And I shall add a fourth stage, of Verification . . . in which both the validity of the idea was tested, and the idea itself was reduced to exact form.[7]

Craig Skinner has helped us by giving a preacher-friendly version of this process which he labels the creative cycle of: informing, exploring, withdrawing, discovering, and verifying. In the informing part of the cycle, we are to fill our minds with as many ideas

---

6. Gabora, "Creativity," 1.
7. Wallas, *The Art of Thought*, 80, 81.

or facts related to the issue at hand as possible without passing judgment as to their relevance. The exploring stage is the agonizing one where every possible association between the various ideas and facts unearthed above is investigated. This is the hard part of "wonder working" and often ends in frustration. This necessitates the next stage which is withdrawing. At this point our work is to be totally abandoned to the inner creative self and we are to occupy our conscious minds with other tasks and allow our subconscious minds to work underground. This may require several days. Next is the stage of discovering when the creative ideas begin to pop out of "nowhere." There may be several of these and they should be written down immediately, even if they sound a bit off-the-wall. The final stage is that of verifying which allows us to comb through these "hair-brained" ideas and develop the worthy one or ones into full form.[8]

Product.

Theories that highlight the product are the most objective of creativity theories because they tend to be quantitative as well as qualitative and evaluate a person's body of creative work. There are numerous ways to measure creative output[9] but these tend to omit investigating the process of such work and tend to spend their time policing the other theories in terms of their empirical verifiability, so are quite limited for our uses.

Person.

These theories emphasize the qualities of the creative personality. These theories will bear the presuppositions we bring to the understanding of the human personality. We will look at a biblical perspective of human creativity later in this chapter, but there are other ways to view who we are and how we can be creative. Psychoanalytical theories tend to view creativity as some form

---

8. Skinner, "Creativity in Preaching, " 565–68.
9. Plucker and Makel, "Assessment of Creativity," 48–73.

of sublimated sexual energy that is released in creative activity, making creativity almost pathological. Behavioristic approaches would see creativity as a person's capacity to employ previously unconscious understandings in a way that solves an inner tension favorably and possibly leads to receiving positive affirmation for it. This would condition the person to repeat the process. Humanistic understandings of a person would see creativity as less a reaction to base instincts and more a progressive journey to higher levels of self-actualizing behavior.[10]

There are generally accepted qualities that are identified as components in the creative personality. J.P. Guilford has contended that divergent thinking (the opposite of convergent, or conventional thought) is characterized by fluency in thinking (in the use of words, ideas, associations and expression), flexibility in thinking, originality and the ability to elaborate.[11] Gregory Feist suggests that the most common traits of the creative personality are: openness to experience, conscientiousness, self-acceptance, hostility, and impulsivity. Those whose creativity is expressed in more scientific endeavors tended to score higher in areas of conscientiousness and self-acceptance than those of a more artistic bent.[12] From this research, we might imagine pictures of the creative personality that could have both positive and negative spiritual, personal and social implications. The creative preacher need not become an arrogant, driven, impulsive libertine. Creativity within the bounds of a growing spiritual relationship through Jesus Christ can give a positive expression to the preacher open to wonder and cause wonder within God's "wonder-full" creation.

Ways in which we might enhance our creative personality abound. Authors you may want to investigate with a discerning eye are Roger von Oech and Julia Cameron. Von Oech is a business consultant and Cameron is a writer. Their works reflect their own presuppositions which are not always congruent with a historic Christian perspective, but have enough that is helpful to say that

10. Bergquist, "A Comparative View of Creativity Theories," 1, 2.

11. Guilford, *The Nature of Human Intelligence*, 138.

12. Feist, "A Meta-analysis of the Impact of Personality on Scientific and Artistic Creativity," 290–309.

warrants careful reading. Von Oech, for instance, encourages us to increase our creativity by developing our explorer (the capacity to search for new information), our artist (the capacity to turn existing resources into new ideas), our judge (the capacity to evaluate the merits of an idea), and our warrior (the capacity to put new ideas into action).[13] Along with these roles of the creative personality, von Oech also highlights a list of axioms that he terms as whacks to the side of the head to release our capacity to think creatively (in paraphrased form):

1. Don't just look for *the* right answer, but many right answers.
2. Use metaphorical thinking in the imaginative phase and logic in the practical phase of creative thought.
3. Breaking the rules or destruction can often lead to creative construction.
4. Premature evaluation can prevent conception.
5. Use play to fertilize your thinking.
6. Do not narrow your focus or limit your field of view.
7. Reverse your perspective or play the fool in order to generate creative alternatives.
8. Cultivate ambiguity in order to stimulate your imagination.
9. Don't be afraid to fail.
10. Believe that you are creative.[14]

Julie Cameron has a trilogy of books designed to help develop a sense of creativity: *The Artist's Way: A Spiritual Path to Higher Creativity* (1992), *Walking in This World: The Practical Art of Creativity* (2002), and *Finding Water: The Art of Perseverance* (2006). Cameron's books surface in all kinds of creative contexts, so even though she betrays a bit of a panentheistic bent, there is much to learn from the pages of these books.

---

13. Von Oech, A *Kick in the Seat of the Pants*, 11–21.
14. von Oech, A *Whack on the Side of the Head*, 33–226.

Place.

Theories related to place investigate the setting or climate in which a person resides. Some aspects of a setting may encourage creativity and some may hinder it. Many developmental theories of creativity take the person's environment, especially family environment, into account as an important factor in the expression of creative thinking and activity. For instance, parents who are themselves creative and who allow their children to be exposed to diverse experiences often have creative children. Issue of family structure and dynamics (e.g. birth order, family size, socio-economic level and neighborhood) may also be factors in fostering a creative place.[15] Obstacles to the development of creativity might include: significant trauma such as loss of a parent or sibling, repression of thought, overscheduling and busyness which leads to an over-emphasis upon academic and athletic achievement and under-emphasis upon creative play.[16] It is a concern that our family and academic environments may be discouraging creativity rather than encouraging it. This has prompted social critic Neil Postman to remark, "Children enter school as question marks and leave as periods."[17]

Raymond Nickerson provides a helpful summary of what should be included in fostering a creative environment:

1. Establishing purpose and intention—a long term deep and abiding purposefulness to develop one's creative potential.
2. Building basic skills—strengthening the skills that lead to creative expression (e.g. language, mathematics, problem solving, self-direction).
3. Encouraging acquisitions of domain-specific knowledge—mastering the knowledge of the field in which creative expression is the goal.
4. Stimulating and rewarding curiosity and exploration—finding ways to encourage childlike forms of playfulness and curiosity.

---

15. Kozbelt, et al., "Theories of Creativity," 26.
16. Russ and Fiorelli, "Developmental Theories of Creativity," 242–44.
17. Von Oech, *A Whack on the Side of the Head*, 35.

5. Building motivation—especially internal motivation and passion for creative expression.
6. Encouraging confidence and a willingness to take risks—counteracting fear of failure and building up confidence to take necessary risks.
7. Focusing on mastery and self-competition—more attention paid to competing against one's own past performance.
8. Promoting supportable beliefs about creativity—instilling the belief that effort and enthusiasm can help creativity develop.
9. Providing opportunities for choice and discovery—allowing personal choice to factor into the areas of study and creative expression.
10. Developing self-management—paying attention to one's own thought processes and taking responsibility for self-evaluation.
11. Teaching techniques and strategies for facilitating creative performance—studying the techniques of creative problem solving.
12. Providing balance—strike the appropriate balance between freedom and structure, spontaneity and self-restraint.[18]

When all this has been said, we are really not much closer to unmasking the secrets of wonder. Jonah Lehrer sums it up by saying:

> The mystery is this: although the imagination is inspired by the everyday world—by its flaws and its beauties—we are able to see beyond our sources, to imagine things that exist only in the mind. We notice an incompleteness and we can complete it: the cracks in things become a source of light. . . . Every creative story is different. And every creative story is the same. There was nothing. Now there is something. It's almost magic.[19]

---

18. Nickerson, "Enhancing Creativity," 408–19.
19. Lehrer, *Imagine*, 252–53.

A "Theolory" of Wonder

As poetic as Lehrer's comments might seem, to say there was nothing and then there is something, brings us to the need for a theology of wonder, especially as it relates to the biblical doctrine of creation.

A THEOLOGY OF WONDER

Wonder has quite a past. Warren Weirsbe summarizes this long history by suggesting Plato thought imagination destroyed reality (because it just came up with imitations of earthly things which themselves were only copies of the ideal things), Judaism was worried imagination would threaten reality (because of their propensity to make images and idols), medieval Christians warned that imagination could distract from true reality, the Renaissance thought imagination could create reality and today many think imagination helps to interpret reality.[20] Over the years, at different times, wonder has been seen as a purely divine ability, as a somewhat questionable human dalliance, and as a quantifiable human capacity. Our task is to uncover a distinctively Christian understanding of wonder that does justice to its divine sources and its human expression. We will assume most of the theological groundwork has been laid in the previous chapter so that will allow us to give more attention to the doctrine of creation.

God the Father, Creator of Heaven and Earth.

We can color our worldview by our own vocabulary. Words are powerful and, dare we say, creative. By referring to God as Creator and to what he has made as Creation, we commit ourselves to a perspective that not only interprets our understanding of God and the world but also has implications for creativity or wonder. This vocabulary takes us from a world dominated by left-brained analysis and opens us to a new life animated by our relationship to our loving Creator who has enveloped us in his creative handiwork. We are returned to our rightful role of a worshipping creature made in

---

20. Wiersbe, *Preaching and Teaching with Imagination*, 321, 322.

the image of the One who creates. Sometimes a change in perspective is all the jump start we need.

Before we look at the respective roles of the Father, Son and Holy Spirit in creation, we need to be reminded that creation is an act of the triune God. Karl Barth reminds us that ". . . God the Creator is the triune God, Father, Son and Holy Spirit. . . . Hence the proposition that God the Father is the Creator and God the Creator the Father can be defended only when we mean by "Father" the "Father with the Son and the Holy Spirit.""[21] Crassly put, all of what we see has been created by all of God, together. Traditionally we confess that the Father creates the world through the Son, by his Spirit.

As we look at the role of the Father in creation, whom we term the Principal (or primary or direct agent) of creation, we'll adopt what Alec Motyer calls the Creation Quadrilateral—"the four-sided reality of the Creator's activity: originating, maintaining, controlling and directing."[22]

Originator.

We confess that God the Father has brought all things into being. The Bible begins with the stark assertion, "In the beginning, God created the heavens and the earth" (Gen 1:1). This is a wide claim that does not stop to tease out the details of all it states. The rest of Scripture is a commentary, in one way or another, of this initial verse. Traditionally, we have referred to God's act of creation as free and loving.

What does it mean when we speak of creation as "free"? For the act of creation to be free, God could not be driven or forced to create by some external force or internal compulsion. Stan Grenz explains: "God is fully himself within the divine Trinity apart from the world in that God is love within himself as the Triune One. Consequently, the existence of the universe comes about through a

---

21. Barth, *The Doctrine of Creation*, III.I, 48, 49.
22. Motyer, *Look to the Rock*, 161.

A "Theolory" of Wonder

free act, and not by necessity."[23] This free and gracious act is most often interpreted as an expression of God's sovereignty; that he was not forced to create. While this is true, many have missed the connection between freedom and playfulness. In fact, as we have seen, freedom is the essence of playfulness. Free creation may indeed exhibit a sovereign God but also a playful one, one who created the world "for no apparent reason."[24] In fact, one way to describe creation, since the world was spoken into existence (Gen 1:3, 6, 9, 14, 20, 24; Heb 11:3), is as primordial word play. At the climax of creation, the forming of humanity, we see examples of word play in both the name of the man (Gen 2:7) and the woman (Gen 3:20) and in the relationship between the genders (Gen 2:23).[25] Along with the biblical witness to God's word as expressing creative power (Pss 33:6; 104:7; 148:5; Isa. 41:4; 44:26; 48:13; Amos 9:6; John 1:1; Rom 4:17; 2 Cor 4:6; Heb 11:3), we see a certain holy playfulness in action. Then we are free ourselves to sense the poetic feel of the creation account and appreciate the lyrical interpretation of creation found in Psalm 104.

To understand the playfulness within creation is not to deny the serious side of the issue or to assert that God acted irrationally or irresponsibly in creation. It is a basic attempt to understand reality. Creation gives answers to foundational questions of identity and purpose and to misinterpret creation is to misinterpret life. So if the playful side of creation is recognized, especially the playful aspect of the Creator himself, a more balanced view of life under this Creator can be realized. It is simply to ask:

> Is there no joy and delight in creating, no sense of creating for the sake of creating? Is this creative labor not also a marvelous form of play, a prodigious frolicking of whirling galaxies and whirling atoms and whirling whirligigs? Are the gyrations of the planets, or the ponderous steps of elephants, or the dartings of little fishes actually to be construed as gravely serious motions? Are swarming bees and burrowing gophers and nest-building

---

23. Grenz, *Theology for the Community of God*, 130.
24. Cf. Moltmann, *Theology of Play*, 16, 17.
25. Bullard, "Biblical Humor," 83.

birds really so hard at work? Is this great drama not also something of a great comedy, so that to fail to see it in both modes is to miss something of special significance and lose an important dimension of life?[26]

A free creation is related to a creation out of nothing. When the Father spoke the heavens and the earth into being, he was all that existed. In a free act of creation, God chooses to create something other than himself, ". . . in creation God chooses "something" and rejects "nothing." God rejects the nothingness of the void. He willfully says "no" to non-existence."[27]

A free creation also relates to a loving creation since God does not have to overcome a basic reluctance to create for fear of diminishing himself. Our God is not a self-absorbed egotist who desires to contemplate himself eternally. His nature is self-giving love and so he does not act "out of character" in creating the heavens and the earth. "The act of creation is the outflowing of the eternal love relationship within the triune God. The world exists because out of the overflow of his own character, which is love, the eternal God establishes an external counterpart, creation."[28]

We notice something else about God's creative activity. Some of it is the act of bringing into being. The word used in Genesis 1:1 for "created" (*bara*) is only used with God as its subject. God alone has the power to bring something out of nothing without the use of existing materials—an immediate creation or a *creatio immediata*. But God also has the capacity to make or form or fashion out of already existing matter (Gen 1:25, 26). This brings order, shape and symmetry out of what was lesser and often chaotic—a creation through means or a *creatio mediata*. So God's creative capacities have both these qualities: a bringing into being and a shaping into something, both a fiat and a forming. Millard Erickson explains:

> The description of the forming of man suggests the use of some type of material—"dust from the ground" (2:7). Eve is described as being formed from a part of the body

26. Hyers, *The Meaning of Creation*, 191.
27. Grenz, *Theology for the Community of God*, 132.
28. Ibid., 133.

A "Theolory" of Wonder

of Adam (2:21). So also God formed every beast of the field and every bird of the air from the ground (2:19). It may well be that what God did originally was merely to create matter from nothing, and then in his subsequent creative activity, he fashioned everything from the atoms which he had created. The various species produced at a later time would be just as much God's doing as was the origin of matter.[29]

Maintainer.

There is a continuing relationship between the God who brought the heavens and the earth into being and the One who watches over all he has made. There is nothing in the Bible about God as the divine watchmaker who winds up creation and then abandons it to take a licking until it stops ticking. God is personally involved with what he has made, maintaining it and watching over it with the doting diligence of a loving parent. This is normally what we refer to as God's providential care over creation. Barth explains: "What we shall have to understand specifically as God's providence, as the preservation and government of man and the world by Him, is also creation, continuing creation, *creatio continua*."[30] What should strike us about this aspect of creation is that it is ongoing—something foundational to an understanding of wonder.

Controller and Director.

The first of these deals with God's sovereign control over all he has made. The second relates to God's ability to direct creation toward his eschatological purposes. Both of these are well worth further study but do not have the same relevance for our understanding of wonder.

---

29. Erickson, *Christian Theology*, 373.
30. Barth, *The Doctrine of Creation*, III.I, 60.

His Name Shall be Wonderful Creator

There is no direct mention of the involvement of God the Son in the Genesis account of creation. The reason for this would appear obvious. However, what is only hinted at in the Old Testament (e.g. if we employ a Christological interpretation of wisdom's role in creation in Proverbs 8), is trumpeted in the New Testament.

> In the beginning was the Word, and the Word was with God, and the Word was God. He was in the beginning with God. All things were made through him, and without him was not any thing made that was made. In him was life, and the life was the light of men. The light shines in the darkness, and the darkness has not overcome it. . . . He was in the world, and the world was made through him, yet the world did not know him (John 1:1–5, 10).

> For although there may be so-called gods in heaven or on earth—as indeed there are many "gods" and many "lords"— yet for us there is one God, the Father, from whom are all things and for whom we exist, and one Lord, Jesus Christ, through whom are all things and through whom we exist (1 Cor 8:5, 6).

> He is the image of the invisible God, the firstborn of all creation. For by him all things were created, in heaven and on earth, visible and invisible, whether thrones or dominions or rulers or authorities—all things were created through him and for him. And he is before all things, and in him all things hold together (Col 1:15–17).

> Long ago, at many times and in many ways, God spoke to our fathers by the prophets, but in these last days he has spoken to us by his Son, whom he appointed the heir of all things, through whom also he created the world. He is the radiance of the glory of God and the exact imprint of his nature, and he upholds the universe by the word of his power (Heb 1:1–3a).

We saw God the Father as the Principal of creation—we might see God the Son as the Principle of creation. The Father is the one who created all things and the Son is the one through whom all

A *"Theology" of Wonder*

things were created—an indirect agent in relation to a direct agent. The Son serves as the unitive principle of creation through whom creation took place and to whom all creation is directed. Of all that might be said about Jesus in this light, we'll focus only on three descriptions most germane to our study of wonder: Jesus as the Word of God, Jesus as the Image of God and Jesus as the Word made flesh.

Jesus as the Word of God.

Preachers cannot deny the importance of Jesus being described as the Word. That Jesus as the Word is connected to creation makes it doubly significant. For John to speak of Jesus this way in the prologue to his gospel connects Jesus with God's work of creation at least in the two senses of origination and maintenance we discussed above. As interesting as "word" (*logos*) is in its Greek philosophical context, John is connecting primarily with its Old Testament pedigree. "There [in the Old Testament], 'the word' (Heb. dabar) of God is connected with God's powerful activity in creation (*cf.* Gn. 1:3ff.; Ps. 33:6), revelation (Je. 1:4; Is. 9:8; Ezk. 33:7; Am. 3:1, 8) and deliverance (Ps. 107:20; Is. 55:1). . . . God simply speaks, and his powerful word creates."[31] John completes his prologue by saying, "No one has ever seen God; the only God, who is at the Father's side, he has made him known" (1:18). Referring to Jesus as the Word, highlights his role in both creation and revelation. Both of these roles are foundational for a theology of wonder.

Jesus as the Image of God.

Paul refers to Jesus as "the image of the invisible God" in his beautiful hymn to the Colossians (cf. 2 Cor 4:4). We hear the same echoes of the creation account in this term (Gen 1:26) and see a connection to revelation as well since many connect the term "image" (*eikon*) with the revelatory role of "wisdom" in Proverbs 8:22: "The Lord possessed me [wisdom] at the beginning of his work, the first of his acts of old." Peter O'Brien states, ". . . "image" emphasizes

31. Carson, *The Gospel According to John*. 115.

Christ's relation to God. The term points to his revealing of the Father on the one hand and his pre-existence on the other—it is both functional and ontological."[32] The use of "image" in relation to Jesus has a significant connection to our concern with wonder. Dorothy Sayers explains:

> Something, which, by being an image, expresses that which it images. . . . There is something that is, in the deepest sense of the words, unimaginable, known to itself (and still more, to us) only by the image in which it expresses itself through creation; and, says Christian theology very emphatically, the Son, who is the express image, is not the copy, or imitation, or representation of the Father, nor yet inferior or subsequent to the Father in any way. In the last resort, in the depths of their mysterious being, the unimaginable and the image are one and the same.[33]

So the use of "image," related as it is to "imagination," is more than merely representation, but also revelation.

Jesus as the Word Made Flesh.

The Incarnation has considerable implications for an understanding of wonder. The fact that Jesus humbled himself by becoming a man (Phil 2:6, 7) underscores the inherent goodness of creation (Gen 1:31). If all creation was inherently evil, God could hardly become part of his creation and not be tainted by it. For this reason, the Incarnation has been the bedrock for a Christian understanding of wonder or creativity.

We need to take care, in the process of vindicating wonder, that we don't do it at the expense of the uniqueness of Christ's incarnation. The Word made flesh cannot and should not serve as the justification of all kinds of unsavory creative activities. Leland Ryken warns us:

---

32. O'Brien, *Colossians, Philemon*, 44.
33. Sayers, *The Whimsical Christian*, 84.

A "Theolory" of Wonder

> There has been a one-sided emphasis on the Incarnation in Christian aesthetic theory to the neglect of other doctrines. One often gets the impression that to affirm every facet of earthly life, including sin, is to follow the pattern of Christ. Yet Christ rejected as well as affirmed earthly life. He said some thoroughly uncomplimentary things about physical reality and earthly endeavor.[34]

The Principle of Creation in Action.

If we have highlighted the role Jesus plays in creation, can we find examples of his own creativity while he pitched his tent among us? There is an embarrassing wealth of examples for us to note, so we will only mention three: parables, poetry and word pictures (images).

Jesus' preferred method of teaching is through the use of parables. These stories display the height of creativity on Jesus' part. Disguised as small vignettes taken from everyday life, Jesus would booby trap them with some life-altering truth about the Kingdom of God. They were like velvet covered hand grenades—warm and fuzzy on the outside but full of explosive power on the inside. Part of the rhetorical impact of his parables has to do not only with the amount of imagination he used to tell them, but the appeal he made to the imagination of his hearers. Jeff Arthurs notes, "Parables express truth concretely, not abstractly, and the realism sparks our imaginations. Vivid and concrete stories transport us to the rugged wilderness and a dark home."[35]

Jesus employed Hebrew poetry in his teaching as well. There is hardly a more creative genre than poetry, even if we do not naturally understand the genius of biblical poetry. The major feature of biblical poetry, of course, is parallelism. A few examples may whet your appetite to look for more in the gospels. Jesus used: synonymous parallelism: "If a kingdom is divided against itself, that kingdom cannot stand. And if a house is divided against itself, that house will

---

34. Ryken, *The Liberated Imagination*, 17.
35. Arthurs, *Preaching with Variety*, 108.

not be able to stand" (Mark 3:24, 25); antithetical parallelism: "One who is faithful in a very little is also faithful in much, and one who is dishonest in a very little is also dishonest in much" (Luke 16:10); synthetic parallelism: "I came to cast fire on the earth, and would that it were already kindled! I have a baptism to be baptized with, and how great is my distress until it is accomplished! Do you think that I have come to give peace on earth? No, I tell you, but rather division" (Luke 12:49–51; climactic parallelism: "Whoever receives one such child in my name receives me, and whoever receives me, receives not me but him who sent me" (Mark 9:37); and chiasmus: "Whoever exalts himself will be humbled, and whoever humbles himself will be exalted" (Matt 23:12).

Jesus also used images and vivid word pictures in his teaching. A representative, but not exhaustive list of pictures used by Jesus would include: shepherd, vipers, fishers of men, door, eye, bridegroom, cross, whitewashed tombs, salt, light, reed, lambs, wolves, baptism, temple, manna, wine, bread, vine, and seed.[36]

The Creative Spirit

The Holy Spirit also has a role in creation. In turn with the Father as the Principal of creation and the Son as the Principle of Creation, the Holy Spirit might be termed the Power of creation. God's Spirit (*ru'ach*) was the life-giving power present at creation (Gen 1:2). The Spirit brought life to creatures (Gen 2:7; 6:3, 17; Job 33:4; Ps 104:30) in relation to the creative work of the Father and Son. Stan Grenz notes, "The creation of the world comes as the outflowing of the eternal love relationship within the triune God. . . . the Spirit is the personal power of God—the dynamic of love between the Father and the Son—by means of which all things exist."[37]

---

36. Wiersbe, *Preaching and Teaching with Imagination*, 166–69.
37. Grenz, *Theology for the Community of God*, 138, 139.

A "Theory" of Wonder

Homo Admirans (wondering man)

Humans are created in the image of God (Gen 1:26). Those who belong to Christ are being changed into his image (2 Cor 3:18, Col 3:10). This was discussed in the previous chapter, but it remains to be seen how this image relates to our capacity to create. Sam Keen states:

> That man is created in the image of God means that he is given lordship over the earth. Within the limits of the givenness [sic] of finite experience, man gives structure and meaning to his world. Man is a creator of meaning and value. As a creature, he must discover and accept the meaning implicit in the world into which he emerges, but as one created in the image of God, man is a creator of meaning. Thus man's creative potential is real but not unlimited; it is his responsibility to complete the creation of a world that has been turned over to him....[38]

We might express the role of human creativity as co-creativity, but that would be over-stepping the limitations of our creaturely status. We are best to claim sub-creativity and that by God's invitation and though his direction.[39] We are invited to bring our God-given capacities to create and imagine, since "imagination, too, belongs no less legitimately in its way to the human possibility of knowledge."[40]

This is not to say our capacity to create is unhindered by sin. Our creative capacities can be used either to glorify or grieve God. In the same way that God gifted Bezalel to create works of art to aid in worship (Exod 31-1-11), he was also grieved by the work of the hands of his people (Isa 66:18; Jer 32:30). In the same way that God is praised through music all through the Bible, he can also demand them to stop their hypocritical musical worship (Amos 5:23). We develop a Christian imagination by steering clear of the two extremes of either condemning it completely as idolatrous or worshipping it as a vestige of the divine image. The last word goes

---

38. Keen, *Apology for Wonder*, 84.
39. Stevens, *The Other Six Days*, 97.
40. Barth, *The Doctrine of Creation*, III.I, 91.

to Janine Langan: "The imagination is not its own end, just as art is not for art's sake. It is an instrument of encounter, at the service of life—one's own and that of others."[41]

After we have come this far, we now have time to stop and reflect over our journey to this point. Our attempts at creative and humorous communication of the Bible need a theological foundation. That is what we have attempted over these last two chapters. The more practical matters of "now what" and "how to" are outside waiting to join the party.

---

41. Langan, "The Christian Imagination," 76.

3 | The Use of Wit in Sermon Development

IF YOU HAVE PERSEVERED this far, you are to be congratulated. You have waded through all the sections on theology and theory and have finally arrived at the business end of all this wit and wonder stuff. Or . . . you might be one of those overly practical types and have skipped over the past few chapters just to get to the "plug and play" parts. If that is the case, go directly to jail and do not collect $200. Don't say I didn't warn you! Knowing "how" without knowing "why" doesn't make you a wise steward of your time, it makes you dangerous—like a cross-eyed javelin thrower. However, if you insist, just be aware that a few more practical ideas will last as long as it takes either to use or discard them and you won't have a way of coming up with your own. You are buying frozen fish fillets instead of learning how to fish.

With my soapbox out of the way, let's get down to business. The heavy lifting is done but we still need to show why and how wit comes into play in the development of the sermon itself. If you can picture a funnel in your mind's eye, we are now working our way down to the narrow part of it where it becomes focused on the matter at hand—using wit in developing the sermon. What we have established in general terms, we now apply specifically to preaching. We agree with Haddon Robinson who says, "Since preaching deals with life, it has to have some element of humor. We have to look at life as it's lived and see at times how absurd it is."[1] We'll start with the reasons to use wit in sermons and then get around to ways this might be done.

REASONS FOR USING WIT IN PREACHING

Don't worry if this is starting to sound theoretical again. We need to show the value wit brings to preaching before finding ways of incorporating it into our sermon preparation regimen. There are many reasons that wit is fit for preaching—you could probably add some of your own—but we will highlight these eight:

The Bible has a lot of wit in it.

This doesn't need proving any longer since we've shown, at least to some degree, that wit is not foreign to the contents and message of Scripture but is woven into its very fabric. There is not a form of biblical literature where humour is completely absent (even in apocalyptic literature, if you look closely enough). Our issue is perception. We have been prompted to think wit is beneath the sacred intentions of Scripture and so we might miss what God has woven right into his Word. It is possible for someone to read the entire Bible and not see anything humorous, but that says more about the one doing the reading than what is read. The preacher needs to look for all God is saying in a particular text—including the possibility of humorous aspects—if exegesis is being done properly.

A proper hermeneutic is a holistic one that listens to the text intently and not through preconceived parameters that count out *a priori* some of what might be contained in the text. Some critical scholars adopt what they call a hermeneutic of suspicion which automatically puts the preacher at odds with the text or the informing presuppositions behind the text. Other preachers may not use a hermeneutic of suspicion, but more of a hermeneutic of solemnity, so they think lemons and prunes are the fruit of the Spirit and wouldn't be able to see anything witty in a given text even

---

1. Beukema, "Why Serious Preachers Use Humor," 131.

The Use of Wit in Sermon Development

if it jumped out and bit them on the nose (I am aware of the opposite extreme of those who see wit everywhere—even where it is absent, More on that later in this chapter). What we need is a new, fuller hermeneutic—a "humourneutic"—that opens up this aspect of Holy Scripture to us. Whether it is the prophet Isaiah railing at the stupidity of worshipping worthless idols, or Elijah mocking the prophets of Baal on Mount Carmel, or Paul's use of biting irony as he writes to the Corinthians, many biblical texts cannot be wholly understood without paying attention to the humorous dimension. If you can recall back to chapter 1, the entire meta-narrative of Scripture has a comedic structure. That being the case, we shouldn't be surprised to find wit scattered throughout its pages. All this to say: the Bible contains wit, preachers are to preach what the Bible says, therefore . . . well, you do the math.

Wit is able to communicate truth.

Part of the value of wit is that it does speak the truth. Often wit can make a point that rings true and that is part of why it's so powerful. Wit unmasks our human frailties and unearths our impure motives and our unhealthy desires and behaviors. Wit can take no prisoners because it labels what people know to be the case. Wit displays the human condition, warts and all, in a way that makes us both sit up and listen and bend over with laughter. If you take the time to analyze the acts of most comedians, you'll find most of their material comes from their everyday experiences. We laugh at them because we identify with what they are saying. As the old proverb states: "Many a true word is spoken in jest." The wise preacher knows some truths that are best spoken this way. Not all wit is supposed to be "funny ha ha;" some of it can be "funny aha"—the wit of a new discovery. Because wit often structures the bare facts and may stretch them or even fabricate them at times, doesn't mean it cannot be a vehicle of the truth. Jesus made up all kinds of stories to communicate the truth—we call them parables. We are in good company.

With Wit and Wonder

Wit helps the preacher establish rapport and relationship with and within the congregation.

It is hard to listen to a stranger. We are more prone to listen to someone who has something in common with us. We listen to people who speak our language. Often the preacher is at a distinct vocational disadvantage because many congregants feel a large chasm between themselves and the clergy—even their own clergy. Some (who don't listen to the news) might feel that preachers are completely pure and don't have the same issues as the rest of them in the congregation. Many may wonder what the preacher might say that could possibly be relevant to their lives. Add to this the reputation that many preachers are so heavenly minded that they're no earthly good, and you can have a significant communication barrier. Preachers need to connect with the congregation and help the congregation to connect with each other. Here is where wit is particularly helpful.

Humour is the *lingua franca* of our culture. Wit is highly prized among us. There is hardly a soul who doesn't want to have a sense of humour—even those who don't seem to have one. Wit is everywhere—in common conversation, in all forms of media including commercials, social media and even (sometimes) in television sit-coms. A person without a sense of humour seems out of touch with the way life is in our culture. Humourless people seem unable to deal with the reality of life and the frailties of humanity. If the congregation can laugh with you as the preacher, you have bridged the communication chasm. Wit shows you know their language, you live on the same planet as they do and you might just be someone who could speak truth into their lives. Laughing together is part of the glue of community. And when the congregation joins in laughing with the preacher, they are also joining in laughing with each other. Wit can build this sense of community and so becomes a valuable instrument in the hands of a faithful preacher who will not misuse its power.

Rapport can be a slippery thing. The preacher who preaches regularly to the same congregation will need to spend less time establishing this connection (at least with most of the congregation—there will always be at least a few members who are longing for either your predecessor or your successor). Life together should help to establish a sense of community. But this can never be taken for granted. Preaching through a time of serious conflict in the local church and preaching to unfamiliar audiences puts even more pressure on the preacher to establish this rapport. To be able to use wit well in these circumstances—to show you speak their language but in a way that is not self-promoting but tastefully self-deprecating—will help to open the lines of communication.

Wit helps to capture and keep the attention of the congregation.

If we assume everyone in the congregation arrives on Sunday morning after a fitful sleep due to their giddy anticipation of what we will be saying, we need our medications adjusted. If we once had such a dream, reality takes little time to burst that bubble. The sheer "dailyness" of life means that each member and visitor on a given Sunday morning comes with all kinds of thoughts and feelings crowding their minds, each vying for center stage. They have personal, interpersonal, financial, ethical, and emotional issues ringing in their ears as they enter the worship space. Each worshipper is a collection of "rabbit trails" just waiting to happen. Into this chaos, we stand to preach. John Drakeford reminds us of the old recipe for rabbit stew that begins with the instructions, "First catch a rabbit."[2] Wit can help with this rabbit trap.

The first few moments of the sermon need to be arresting to the congregation. Arresting in the sense that they are probably heading in another direction and you need to give them good reason to head in yours. Advertisers know the value of wit in capturing attention and so preachers can learn something from them (remembering that a sermon is not a lengthy commercial). This is not to say preachers should begin every sermon with wit, or the proverbial funny-but-not-in-the-least-related-to-the-sermon-theme joke. This is counterproductive because it is predictable. Predictability is

---

2. Drakeford, *Humor in Preaching*, 30.

lethal. Wit includes incongruity or surprise. Predictable wit is an oxymoron.

Added to the challenge of capturing people's attention is that of keeping or recapturing it. Attention spans are shrinking at an alarming rate and now are measured in seconds rather than minutes. There are crying babies, screeching hearing aids, bathroom parades and ever-present smart phones beckoning everyone to either check your biblical references, check the scores or their favorite social media sites. Incidences of ADD and ADHD are climbing and seem to affect everyone in one way or another. During the span of a sermon, there will be times when members of the congregation will tune you out and follow their own rabbit trails. This happens in different ways and at different times with each person, but rest assured it will happen. Sometimes it's something you say that sends them off (and some of those occasions can be inspired by the Spirit who is using your words to make his point), or they might be distracted by some external stimulus. To have some witty "attention re-gathering" strategies planned for different parts of the sermon can be helpful here. Also, the preacher needs to be ready for those surprises that may be large scale disruptions. Not all these can and should be dealt with by wit—such as medical emergencies in the midst of the sermon—but often a well-timed witty response can refocus attention from the elephant in the room back to the sermon. Be careful, however, not to overcompensate by making too much of the distraction, no matter how witty your rejoinder might be. You need to name the elephant in the room, not ride it. You want to bring the congregation back and not send them away somewhere else.

Wit overcomes defenses and increases receptivity.

Sometimes the issue is not so much building bridges to the faithful but breaking down barriers for the anxious and antagonistic. Some listeners may be more than scattered in their thoughts—their thoughts might be shattered. Wit can ease some of these tensions so they can feel at ease and become open to what the preacher is

The Use of Wit in Sermon Development

saying. Preachers should not assume a level playing field as far as receptivity to the gospel is concerned. Some present in worship are hurting seriously—marital, familial, financial or health challenges may be causing them to despair. Others may be angry at others, themselves, the church, God or the preacher for what they consider to be a serious offence against them and their well-being. There may be some who are non-believers dragged there by a well-meaning spouse or parent. Some might be overly defensive regarding something in themselves or something they have done. They are not in the mood to hear anything that would challenge what they already know in their heart of hearts to be wrong. It may be hard for either the numb or the stubborn to hear of their need for a Savior.

John Ortberg, a master in the use of wit, shows us how the use of humour can pave the way for everyone to realize their own guilt of sin and need for forgiveness:

> Many years ago, early on in our marriage, my wife and I sold our Volkswagen Beetle to buy our first really nice piece of furniture. It was a sofa. It was a pink sofa, but for that kind of money, it was called a mauve sofa. The man at the sofa store told us all about how to take care of it, and we took it home.
>
> We had very small children in those days, and does anyone want to guess what was the Number One Rule in our house from that day on? "Don't sit on the mauve sofa! Don't play near the mauve sofa! Don't eat around the mauve sofa! Don't touch the mauve sofa! Don't breathe on the mauve sofa! Don't think about the mauve sofa! On every other chair in the house, you may freely sit, but on this sofa—the mauve sofa—you may not sit, for on the day you sit thereon, you will surely die!"
>
> And then one day came the "Fall." There appeared on the mauve sofa a stain . . . a red stain . . . a red jelly stain. My wife called the man at the sofa factory, and he told her how bad that was. So she assembled our three children to look at the stain on the sofa. Laura, who then was about 4, and Mallory, who was about 2 ½, and Johnny who was maybe 6 months. She said, Children, do you see that? That's a stain. That's a red stain. That's a red jelly stain. And the man at the sofa store says it's not coming

> out, not for all eternity. Do you know how long eternity is, children? Eternity is how long we're all going to sit here until one of you tells me which one of you put the red jelly stain on the mauve sofa."
>
> For a long time they all just sat there until finally Mallory cracked. I knew she would. She said, "Laura did it." Laura said, "No, I didn't." Then it was dead silence for the longest time. And I knew that none of them would confess putting the stain on the sofa, because they had never seen their mom that mad in their lives. I knew none of them was going to confess putting the stain on the sofa, because they knew if they did, they would spend all of eternity on the "Time Out Chair." I knew that none of them would confess putting the stain on the sofa, because in fact, I was the one who put the stain on the sofa, and I wasn't sayin' nuthin'! Not a word![3]

Notice the deft use of humorous self-disclosure that allows everyone to see their own need. The truth is, we've all stained the couch and need to confess and be forgiven. Wit can lower these defenses and help to create a greater receptivity to the truths of the gospel. If television sit-coms use laugh tracks to enhance viewer receptivity, surely the weighty truths of Scripture deserve a receptive hearing.

Wit aids in the retention of the sermon.

This is a cumulative effect. If the preacher is able to use wit in the last three ways mentioned above, increased retention of the sermon content should be the result. Drakeford explains:

> First humor captures a student's attention by "tickling his curiosity" about the subject; it frees up attention by releasing stress that might have distracted; and it holds attention by providing motivation and momentum. All this in turn leads to retention.[4]

---

3. Beukema, "Serious Preachers," 134.
4. Drakeford, *Humor*, 12.

The Use of Wit in Sermon Development

This rings true to many preachers. Some congregants may approach the preacher weeks and even years later and recount how a particular bit of wit has stuck with them as an encouragement when they needed it.

Wit contributes to spiritual health.

A humorous perspective not only aids the preacher's growth, but the congregation's as well. Given our human frailties, a healthy response is to take God seriously and ourselves less so. Enjoying some hearty laughter can actually be cathartic and therapeutic. It can restore a gracious perspective to faith as we realize our common dependence upon God. Sometimes we just need a good laugh. As a matter of fact, church health consultant Christian Schwarz notes that a congregation's ability to laugh together is a sign of church health.[5] The medical benefits of laughter are well-documented, the most famous being how Norman Cousins laughed his way back from serious illness to health through a steady diet of watching old black and white comedies.[6] You don't have to be Patch Adams to use the healing power of wit.

One example comes from a time in my own pastoral experience years ago when I pastored a church in a small town. One of our members was named Bob, a vigorous man well into his eighties, known for riding his bicycle all over town. With little notice, Bob grew seriously ill and passed away suddenly. This was a shock to all of us. I told the following story during his funeral service:

> I remember seeing Bob just a couple of weeks ago. I was walking down the sidewalk, heading to the Post Office, when I saw a familiar sight—Bob riding past me on his bicycle. I can recall thinking to myself, "Bob's well over eighty and he's still riding that bike all over town. He should be careful—he could really hurt himself!" Just at that point I happened to trip on a crack in the sidewalk and fell face-first onto the concrete. As I was trying to

---

5. Christian Schwarz, *Natural Church Development,*
6. Norman Cousins, *Anatomy of an Illness.*

pick myself up, feeling a bit sheepish, I noticed that Bob had circled back on his bicycle and was hovering over me. He looked down at me and said, "You should be careful—you could really hurt yourself!"

This was all the excuse we needed. We all had a good cathartic laugh in the midst of our shock and grief.

Wit helps address difficult topics or situations.

Inevitably there come times when a sermon topic, biblical text or a particular situation will contribute to a delicate and difficult preaching task. Simply skipping over it or brushing it under the church carpet screams cowardice. Wit can help the preacher navigate such a situation when used tastefully. Never aim to depreciate the seriousness of the situation, but do not allow the discomfort and anxiety to rob an opportunity for the truth to be told. The preacher never has to go looking for these occasions, they will be plentiful enough as it is. Wit is not the only tool to be used here, but is definitely a part of the preacher's tool kit.

I recall being in the congregation when the guest preacher got up to say he was going to preach about sex. He said he understood that this might be a bit off-putting since sometimes Christians don't know how to handle some of these delicate topics. Then he told us about the last time he preached this same sermon. His topic was announced and then the leader of the service called on one of the elders to lead in prayer before the sermon. This gentleman apparently had not been paying attention to the announcement and so prayed, "O Lord we pray that you will guide the words of the preacher this morning. May we put what he says into practice daily." The ice was broken and the sermon went on from there.

THE LIMITATIONS OF WIT IN A SERMON

In a book like this, you might think wit is a panacea, suitable for all occasions. This is hardly the case. A wise preacher will recognize that, like everything else in our fallen world, wit has some rough edges. Here are some of the common limitations of the use of wit in preaching:

Wit is only the means and not the end.

Some preachers sound like stand-up comics complete with on-stage persona and voice. They are gifted humorists and their messages are a laugh a minute (or more). There can be a danger here of misplaced priorities. For the preacher of the gospel, eliciting "the laugh" cannot be an end in itself. Wit, like everything else, is merely one of the means toward a gospel end. Wit is always to be used in service of the gospel. Whether that is to create rapport so the gospel may be heard, or to capture and maintain attention to the message, or to increase retention, ultimately all wit is to serve the higher end of getting the Word across. If we do not maintain this proper perspective, some preachers may use wit as a way to fulfill their people-pleasing tendencies.

Here is where some preachers and stand-up comics have much in common. Comics live for "the laugh" and when the audience is non-responsive, they normally say they "died" on stage. That language is quite revealing. Laughter is a life-and-death issue for comics. It holds the power over their future employment and their personal well-being. The off-stage behavior of many comics demonstrates this imbalance. Some preachers succumb to this disease. They subtly assume they are successful only when there is lots of laughter and an energetic response to their witty words. We all do well to remember Jesus' warning: "Woe to you, when all people speak well of you, for so their fathers did to the false prophets" (Luke 6:26). Drakeford adds his word of warning: ". . .it is important to remember that a preacher can become too interested in humor, miss the point of his calling, and sink to the role of a jester."[7] The preacher is called to a purpose beyond performance anxiety. Our call is to One far beyond the reaction of crowds and our own over-blown egos. Most of us will never feel the pressure of having to perform regularly in front of massive congregations

7. Drakeford, *Humor*, 93.

or huge convention crowds. It is enough to remain faithful to our calling and use wit wisely in service of the gospel message.

Beware of wit addiction.

Closely related to the above limitation is the danger of wit addiction. Some preachers might climb on the humour train and not want to get off. Such addiction to wit is actually counter-productive, not to mention pathological. While this danger is similar to the one above in result, the motivation is different. The preacher who overuses wit in a pathetic attempt to gain approval is not the same as one who is hooked on humour and cannot stop. Wit addicts aren't near as sensitive to the way they are perceived as to the personal need to get their wit fix. This can exhibit itself in habitual punning, using wit in inappropriate settings, employing inappropriate kinds of humour, and the inability to take anything seriously. This condition, ironically, reverses the attention-getting qualities of wit and actually repels people rather than attract them.

Beware of using wit to express veiled aggression.

Maybe you can remember the Superiority Theory of humour back in chapter 1: we make fun of what is ugly, inferior and unfortunate in others as a way to express our own superiority. We need to guard against this motive in the use of humour in the pulpit. Simply because we can express anger and aggression in a socially-acceptable way, doesn't mean the preacher should stoop this low. Often emotionally-unhealthy preachers can use wit in a sermon to target what they don't have the courage to confront directly—be that a spouse, church board, an annoying or uncooperative church member, or some other issue or situation. Such passive-aggression is a plague in the church and should not be modeled from the pulpit. As a good rule of thumb: never use wit as an escape from dealing directly and pastorally with people or situations.

The Use of Wit in Sermon Development

Do not use inappropriate forms of wit.

Some kinds of wit have no place in the pulpit at all. Forms of humour that degrade a person's gender, nationality, tastes or preferences or that cross the boundaries of appropriate modesty and propriety should be off limits to preachers. Neither is there room for frivolous, flippant forms of wit that add nothing to the communication event except air pollution. Granted, there is great flexibility within these boundaries, given the particular context, but the general principle holds true. There is a vast difference between speaking to the gathered congregation in a formal worship setting on Sunday morning and to a group of college aged students in a retreat or camp setting. The former would generally be more "buttoned down" than the latter, but there are still boundaries that should not be crossed in either or any case. The use of inappropriate wit can not only damage your credibility as a preacher, but be damaging to the church and repute of the gospel as well.

THE USE OF WIT IN PREACHING

Now we turn our attention to the practicalities of employing wit in developing the sermon itself. We will save issues related to the use of wit in the delivery of sermons for the final chapter.

Forms of wit.

You can find a list of humorous forms in Appendix A. We don't need to explain them here, but we do need an understanding of each form and how they communicate as well as how they might best be utilized. As a rule of thumb, you use the form of wit that is suggested by the biblical text itself, your own personality or style of humour and the context in which the sermon is to be delivered. This choice grows easier with practice. The one term that summarizes this best is: contextual. The best wit in a sermon is that which bubbles up out of the text itself, your personality as preacher and the congregational context. In other words, pre-formed, generic or "canned" forms of wit tend to be least effective.

Let me say a word here about the use of jokes in a sermon. By "joke" I mean a self-contained humorous narrative complete with characters and plot twist. These jokes are designed to be funny on their own merits—whether they are heard in another context or read in a printed source. The preacher can decide to insert these jokes into the sermon at various places. Jokes tend to be high risk forms of wit for the preacher. One, if the punch line of the joke does not fit with the lesson it should illustrate, it serves at cross purposes to good communication. It diffuses the point rather than support it. Two, jokes often require a lot of time to tell properly and may take a high percentage of the time you have been given to preach. Three, jokes often require a trademark approach that advertises them in advance. Most congregations can tell when the preacher switches into joke mode. People are waiting for a punch line and some of the surprise that is part of humour is lost—especially if the preacher advertises it with words like, "I heard this funny story last week...." The only thing worse is stopping to explain the joke after it falls flat. If it died the first time, a joke autopsy won't help. This is not to say that jokes are always a bad idea in a sermon. However, they must be used with discretion and discernment.

The timing of wit in the sermon.

You might be wondering when wit should be used in a sermon. The short answer is: at the right times and not all the time. This is not an exact science, to be sure. In terms of the structure of the sermon itself, all else being equal, wit fits best in the introduction of the sermon because it helps establish rapport, captures attention, and eases tensions—all rhetorical tasks to be accomplished in the sermon introduction. Wit may be found at intermitted points in the body of the sermon as befits the message of the text, the preacher's style and the congregational context. Generally speaking, wit should not be prominent in the conclusion of the sermon. Wit, by nature, tends to draw attention to itself and that is often opposed to what the preacher is attempting to do in the conclusion. When wit does support the desired response for the sermon, it can be helpful even in the conclusion.

How to express wit in the sermon.

There are a few essential attitudes in how wit is to be used as part of the sermon development process. They tend to summarize what we have been saying up to this point.

Purposefully.

Wit should be employed to accomplish a particular exegetical, homiletical or rhetorical purpose rather than employed willy nilly at the whim of the preacher. Sometimes, especially if you have a limber funny bone, the hardest task is knowing what wit to exclude rather than looking for something funny to include.

Humbly.

Usually the most effective forms of humour are the ones that demonstrate your own foibles and struggles rather than those of others. Appropriate forms of self-deprecating wit are gracious ways of making a point at your own expense. You lose credibility if you are always the hero. And you lose credibility if you are constantly drawing attention to the issues of others and none of your own. You don't need to worry that other people think you're perfect. Often they're surprised you have a pulse! So loosen up a bit and let them see that you are their fellow pilgrim. Again, this can be overdone. Don't be so self-deprecating that it looks like you are completely incompetent. That doesn't do wonders for your credibility either and really is a subtle form of egocentricity.

Integrally.

Your use of wit should fit who you are as a person. Let your humour flow out of who you are. Everyone has a particular style of wit that fits them and you should determine what that is and learn to be at home there. People can tell when you are trying too hard. Let the style of humour you use in everyday conversation lead you behind the pulpit as well. If you're funny in person, you'll be funny behind the pulpit. If you're not funny in person, don't try to pull a Dr. Jekyll and Mr. Hyde. You can develop your sense of humour, but don't try to do too much too soon.

Honestly.

If you use something witty from another source, find a way to give credit where credit is due. Never try to plagiarize a bit of wit because that is a serious ethical breech. Preachers have lost their credibility and their pulpits for that kind of dishonesty. Besides, if this is from a source that people recognize as funny, it will actually enhance the effect of the wit.

Sensitively.

Always be gracious in the way you use wit in a sermon. Be aware of how various members of the congregation might respond to it. If you realize that a certain piece of wit would be particularly offensive to someone, even if you are dying to use it, try to use pastoral sensitivity in this case. Be aware that it is much easier to transition from something humorous to something serious than the other way around. Be sensitive to your congregation and help them make those transitions appropriately.[8]

---

8. Beukema, "Serious Preachers," 140.

Using Wit Triggers

The most effective wit in sermons is that which fits the content of the biblical text, the style of the preacher and the preaching context. It might be helpful to show how that might be determined. What is it in the text, yourself and the preaching situation that could guide you in the choice of humour for the sermon? We'll look at each of three areas and search for wit triggers that may help you in this planning process. A wit trigger is something that may suggest a certain form or use of wit which fits the occasion. A preacher should be on the lookout for these triggers as the sermon develops.

Textual Wit Triggers

There often are clues in the biblical text itself as to the kind of wit which might be employed. This is most often accomplished by being aware of forms of humour within the text if there are any. Of course not every biblical text contains humorous forms, but once you are aware such forms exist, you might be surprised how often they appear. The most common forms of wit in biblical literature are: irony, satire, invective, sarcasm, parody, travesty, caricature, hyperbole, meiosis, riddle, paradox, proverb, metaphor, simile, rhetorical question, counter question, *a fortiori*, and puns (which are extremely common, especially in the Old Testament, but notoriously hard to detect since we are dealing with English translations of the original languages). You can check Appendix A for definitions of each of these.

Until you become conversant with the various forms of wit, you might begin by asking yourself these questions as you engage the biblical text: does the plain sense of this text make sense?; is there anything odd or surprising about this text? ; how might the original readers have responded to this text?; how would their response be different from mine (or ours)? how might the wit in this text be expressed in our context?

A couple examples from the gospels may help. Suppose you are looking at Mark 10:25: "It is easier for a camel to go through the eye of a needle than for a rich person to enter the kingdom of God." It's hard to take this saying literally, which would trigger the thought it might contain some form of wit. The disciples themselves were astonished by this saying, so that might help us as well (10:26). There is something going on here that suggests a kind of communication that is deeper than its plain sense. Camels were commonly recognized as the largest beasts of burden in Palestine at the time. The eye of a needle was recognized as one of the smallest openings of that time (which was obviously before the advent of nanotechnology). So we have the juxtaposition of two opposites. Jesus' point is that it is easier for this giant beast of burden to squeeze through the eye of a needle than for a rich person to enter God's kingdom. There is obviously a fair bit of shock value to this comparison. It seems like an obvious use of hyperbole—extravagant overstatement to make a point. How might we express this same thought today? There might be a number of ways to express this, depending on your own style of wit and the congregational context. One example might be to look at a semi-trailer truck as a comparable beast of burden and the keyhole as a relatively small opening. You might contemporize the saying today by saying, "It is easier for a Kenworth to drive through a keyhole than for a rich person to enter the kingdom of God." This of course assumes the congregation knows that Kenworth makes semi-trailer trucks.

Look at Luke 11:11–13: "What father among you, if his son asks for a fish, will instead of a fish give him a serpent; or if he asks for an egg, will give him a scorpion? If you then, who are evil, know how to give good gifts to your children, how much more will the heavenly Father give the Holy Spirit to those who ask him!" Jesus is teaching his disciples about prayer in this context and wants to show how readily God desires to give good gifts to his children. The way Jesus poses the rhetorical questions leaves the disciples with no choice but to realize that no father in his right mind would substitute a snake for a fish, or a scorpion for an egg. When children ask their fathers for the simple means of nutrition (e.g. fish and eggs), good fathers would never give them something harmful instead (e.g. snakes and scorpions). Jesus' point is that if earthly fathers know this, then how much more does our heavenly Father. This, then, is an example of *a fortiori* or an arguing from the lesser to the greater. Put into today's terms, we might say, "Which one of you dads, if your child asks for a pizza would give him a landmine; or if your child asks for a grapes, would give him black widow spiders instead?" You might want to dial up or down the severity of the examples depending on your style and the context.

Personal Wit Triggers

The chances of preaching from biblical texts that contain humorous forms are far less than average. How might wit be used in the majority of cases when it is not found directly in the text? Here is where your personal style of wit comes into play. Are you naturally rather wordy in your conversations or do you make every word count? Are you naturally demonstrative in your conversations or restrained? Are you prone to overstatement or understatement? Approachable or guarded? Tigger or Eeyore (Type A or Type B)? Cheerful or somber? Passive or aggressive (not passive-aggressive!)? A leader or a follower? You may not have a clear picture on all these areas of your life, but there are people around you who do. Ask them. Tell them to be honest and then don't blame them when they are.

You will most naturally be drawn to the kinds of wit that fit your personality and style. This is as it should be. Preachers should never try to be someone they are not. That depreciates what God has given each person. He has made us unique for a reason.

Contextual Wit Triggers

These triggers relate to the uniqueness of your particular context. This will change, of course, each time your context changes. You might change venues and audiences, or you might be preaching to the same group long enough to see it change over time. Regardless, you will need to know those you are talking to. Haddon Robinson is fond of saying "The first question of the inexperienced preacher is "What am I to talk about?" while the first question of the experienced preacher is "Who am I talking to?""

With Wit and Wonder

It is best to analyze your context on the macro scale first and then on the micro. Note the larger themes of geography (e.g. West Coast and East Coast are quite different), age (e.g. newer forms of wit tend to be more extreme, absurd and vulgar in the eyes of older people), gender (e.g. males and females have differing appreciations of wit), nationality (e.g. Americans are prone to overstatement and British are prone to understatement; we Canadians can be either, depending on the weather), educational level (e.g. forms of intellectual wit tend to be more subtle and intricate), setting (e.g. morning worship service, secular audience, large group, small group), time (e.g. special occasion, regular occasion, celebration, grieving or shock) and economic level (e.g. blue collar and white collar wit differ as well). After a look at the macro, get specific and analyze the specific group you will be addressing. It will always be unique and you will need to understand their wit threshold. How much will it take to get them engaged and how much is too much or over the line? Sometimes this can only be learned through the process of trial and error, but it is still worth the effort.

William Willimon summarizes the appropriate use of wit in sermons by stating:

> Humor is most effective and justified in preaching when (1) it arises out of interaction of the biblical text with the preacher and the congregation, (2) it is natural for the preacher's own style and personality, (3) the effects of the humor are congruent with the purposes of Christian communication, and (4) the liturgical, congregational context is not violated by the humor.[9]

Willimon gets the last word since he practices what he preaches. We'll conclude this chapter with one of Willimon's sermons—one on a text that includes a humorous form within it. Willimon preached this sermon over twenty years ago in the Duke University Chapel but it still serves as a good example of wit in preaching. He uses examples of textual, personal and contextual wit in the course of the sermon. I will supply commentary in bold letters within square brackets. Enjoy!

---

9. William Willimon, "Humor," 264.

The Use of Wit in Sermon Development

DIVINE DIVESTMENT[10]

> And as he was setting out on his journey, a man ran up and knelt before him and asked him, "Good Teacher, what must I do to inherit eternal life?" And Jesus said to him, "Why do you call me good? No one is good except God alone. You know the commandments: 'Do not murder, Do not commit adultery, Do not steal, Do not bear false witness, Do not defraud, Honor your father and mother.'" And he said to him, "Teacher, all these I have kept from my youth." And Jesus, looking at him, loved him, and said to him, "You lack one thing: go, sell all that you have and give to the poor, and you will have treasure in heaven; and come, follow me." Disheartened by the saying, he went away sorrowful, for he had great possessions.
>
> And Jesus looked around and said to his disciples, "How difficult it will be for those who have wealth to enter the kingdom of God!" And the disciples were amazed at his words. But Jesus said to them again, "Children, how difficult it is to enter the kingdom of God! It is easier for a camel to go through the eye of a needle than for a rich person to enter the kingdom of God." And they were exceedingly astonished, and said to him, "Then who can be saved?" Jesus looked at them and said, "With man it is impossible, but not with God. For all things are possible with God." (Mark 10:17-27)

The Danish philosopher, Soren Kierkegaard, came home after church one Sunday and wrote of his disgust at what happened there:

> In the magnificent cathedral the Honorable and Right Reverend Geheime-General Ober-Hof Pradikant, the elect favorite of the fashionable world, appears before an elect company and preaches with emotion upon the text he himself elected: "God hath elected the base things of the world, and the things that are despised" *and nobody laughs.* (*Attack Upon Christendom*, 1944)

---

10. Willimon, *Peculiar Speech*, 67-74.

With Wit and Wonder

Today I am to preach on Mark 10:17–27. The story of Jesus and the Rich Man. Rick Lischer, Professor of Preaching at the Duke Divinity School, was supposed to preach on this text. I thought that I had asked him to preach on this text on this day. Two weeks ago Rick told me that he had not heard about it, had never received a letter from me, and was planning to be at his fortieth high school reunion. That is no excuse. He was supposed to preach on this text. Now I have to preach on this text. I had to leave my beach house yesterday, get in my $15,000 car, and drive to my $150,000 home, in order to preach to you on this text. [**personal wit—given the age of this sermon, we could easily double the monetary values on his car and home**]

Let us put this episode in context. Jesus has just blessed the children (10:13–16). Jesus was lecturing away one day, everybody trying to pay attention, everybody taking notes on his theology lecture. But his disciples said, "Master, send these children away."

They were being distracted by the children. Somebody had pulled somebody else's hair. Somebody was rolling around in the dirt, wrestling with somebody else. "Master, send these children away."

Do you remember what Jesus did on that occasion? Mark says that he took a child and placed the child in the midst of them. In other words, this helpless, small, ignorant, vulnerable, and dependent little child, the one whom we in our society place at the margins of our society, Jesus put in the midst of them. We put children out on the fringes of our society. After all, they are unproductive, dependent, and vulnerable. We have progressed to the point where our society treats its very young and its very old the same way: namely, we institutionalize them. We put them away in institutions and pay people to look after them. After all, both the very young and the very old make no contribution to society: they are unproductive, dependent, *small.*

The curious thing is that Jesus took those whom we put at the fringe of society and put them right in the middle of the disciples. Those whom we regard as distraction from the really important things, Jesus put in the middle of us in a last ditch effort to help us pay attention.

The Use of Wit in Sermon Development

It's as if Jesus wanted to say, "You want to get into my kingdom? The only way to get into my kingdom is to be very small, very little, very needy. There will be no adults in my kingdom, no self-sufficient, liberated, autonomous, independent adults. There will only be children. Here is a kingdom that has a very small door." At any rate, Jesus has just shocked the disciples by pulling a child out of the crowd and putting the child in the midst of them.

As fate would have it, this episode is followed by another in which anything but a little, weak, needy, dependent, and small child comes forth to Jesus. Mark says the person who came to Jesus was a "rich man." Matthew, when he tells the story, says that he was "young." Luke says that he was a "ruler." But all three Gospels agree that, whether he is young, a ruler, or what, *he is rich*.

This rich man comes to Jesus saying that he wants some of this "Eternal Life" Jesus has to offer. Evidently, despite the fact that he is rich, despite his having many things, he doesn't have "Eternal Life." So he asks Jesus, "What must I *do* to have eternal life?"

What must I do (evidently, he has been very successful at his doing) to get eternal life. "Eternal Life" is just another way of saying "kingdom of God; in Mark's Gospel. "How can I get into your kingdom?" asked the young man who has been very successful at getting to the top of this world's kingdom.

Jesus responds, "You want to get into this kingdom? Simple. All you have to do to get in God's kingdom is to obey all the commandments. Don't worship anything but God, don't commit adultery, don't steal, don't lie, don't kill, don't be envious of anything anybody else has, keep the Sabbath, stuff like that." [**textual**]

Robert Capon says that in invoking the anything-but-simple-to-follow Ten Commandments, Jesus expected this high achiever to recoil and say something like, "Gosh, Jesus, when you put it like that, why in the world should I be going out looking for something else to do, when I have done such a lousy job of doing the things that I have already been commanded to do?"

But this young man was a hard-core success. So he replied, "Gosh, Jesus, I have dome all that since I was a kid in Sunday School." [**textual**] Evidently, this young man is a bigger success than

Jesus thought. He has not only been successful at getting material things but he has been a spiritual success as well.

In the context of that day, the young man's success at keeping the Ten Commandments would not be that surprising. After all, because he is rich, he has plenty of free time on his hands, plenty of time to study the Bible and to do what the Bible commands. If he needs to take all weekend off to study the Bible, go to church, and do good things, he can afford it. It was believed that rich people had been blessed by God. One way they had been blessed is with enough free time to be a success as religion.

I very well remember the woman who told me, when I urged her to come to my church, that she found it difficult to come to church on Sunday morning. When I asked her why, she rather embarrassingly explained, "Look, I am a waitress. I work ten hours a day, six days a week as a waitress. On Sunday morning, when I wake up, I can hardly get out of bed. Worse, my feet are so swollen, I cannot get on my Sunday shoes. That's why I don't come to church."

Because they thought that the rich were blessed with enough free time to read and obey the Bible, hire expensive psychotherapists, go to affluent universities, and ponder the mysteries of life, [contextual] you can imagine their shock when Jesus turns to this materially and spiritually rich young man and says, "So you have succeeded in obeying the Ten Commandments? Then let me ask you to do just one teeny weeny thing for me. Go, sell all you have, and give it to the poor, and come follow me and you treasure in heaven." [textual] To everybody's amazement, Jesus considered the young man's wealth, not as a sign of divine favor, but as a big problem.

"Strip down, raffle your Porsche, liquidate your portfolio, break free and give it all to the poor." [contextual] In other words, strip down, throw away your crutches, become weak, little, small, poor, and vulnerable. You can't get in here, unless you come as a little child. Didn't I say this kingdom has a very small door? With that, Mark says, the young man slumped down, got real depressed, got into his Porsche, and drove away. [contextual]

You see, this is a *call story*. It is very similar to other call stories in the Gospel of Mark (1:16–20; 2:14; 10:46–52). Someone is being

The Use of Wit in Sermon Development

invited to join up with Jesus and become a disciple. Interestingly enough in those stories of Jesus' call and invitation, people come forth and follow. In this story, the man walks away. He walks away because he is rich. As he is walking away, Jesus turns to his disciples (10:23–27), to us, to the church, and says out loud, "Man, it is really hard to get one of these rich ones into my kingdom." One of the disciples says, "How hard is it, Jesus?" [**contextual**]

Jesus says, "It's hard. In fact, I would say it is about as hard for one of these rich people to get into my kingdom as to shove a camel through the eye of a needle." That hard!

Can you see why I wanted Rick Lischer to preach on this text and not me? [**personal**] Let's face it, by the standards of that day, by the standards of this day, we know where we would find our place in this story. *We* are the rich young man. He is us all over. [**contextual**]

Anuradhi Vittachi (Earth Conference One, 1989) asks us to imagine the world as a village with one hundred families:

> If this metaphorical village consists of one hundred families . . . sixty-five cannot read. Some eighty families have no members who have flown on airplanes, and seventy have no drinking water at home. About sixty families occupy ten percent of the village, while just seven own sixty percent of the land. Only one family has a university education.

The rich man is us all over.

And I really wish I could help you out of this "easier for a camel to get through the eye of a needle than for a rich person to enter the kingdom" text. Creative homiletical attempts to change one Greek letter so that the word will not be "camel" but "rope" will not work. Jesus said camel, not rope. (Besides, it would be no easy thing to get a rope through the eye of a needle anyway!) [**textual**] Around the ninth century, some creative preacher claimed that there was a gate in Jerusalem named "The Needle's Eye" so that Jesus was talking about how difficult it was to get a fully loaded camel through this relatively narrow gate. No, that is an invention of a preacher like me who, back in the ninth century, probably had to preach this text to a congregation like us. [**contextual**]

With Wit and Wonder

The disciples spoke for us all, "God! Who can be saved?" And Jesus replies, "It's hard. It's hard. Impossible, for rich people to enter the kingdom. In fact, it is impossible for *anybody* to enter this kingdom. But with God, all things are possible, even this."

Just in case you watched the previous episode with Jesus receiving and blessing the little child (10:13-16) and thought that it was a sweet, nice, easy thing to come to Jesus, Mark records this. We can only come to Jesus as a small, needy, little child. But there's nothing sweet or nice about it. It's hard.

As a preacher, I must not make this sound easy. It's hard. In fact, it is impossible. The Jesus says, "*With God, even this is possible.*" It is even possible who is rich to divest and get into the kingdom. And I don't know whether that is good news or bad. Jesus has clearly taught that you can only come into this kingdom as a child, as someone who is needy, small and poor. How can we come into this kingdom when we are all big, grown up, self-sufficient, well-to-do, and scored high on the SAT? [contextual] Jesus says, "With God it is possible." That is, with God, it is possible that, given enough time, *we* will get stripped down, made small, impoverished, divested.

With God, that is possible? This world's kingdoms belong to those who sing "I Am Just a Material Girl," and "It's Money That Matters." [contextual] You can't imagine the possibility of our being able to let go, strip down, and divest of those things to which we so ruthlessly cling in this life. But with God, Jesus promises, it may be possible. *And I don't know whether that is a promise or a threat.*

As we go through life, getting our advanced degrees, earning our salaries, driving our cars, paying our mortgages, we had better look over our shoulder. When we get all secure, set-up, insured, and well-fixed, there may be that old Pursuer behind us, just waiting to jump us in order to divest us. With God, it's possible. Lamar Williamson says, "If this message does not take our breath away, if we are not shocked, grieved, or amazed, we have either not yet heard it or heard it so often that we do not really hear it anymore."

After we spiritualize it, explain it away, this text sits there, grinning at us. It looks around at us all. We exclaim, "It's hard! Who then can be saved?" With God it may be possible.

The Use of Wit in Sermon Development

She went to Honduras with the Duke Chapel Mission team on her spring break. Went to help the poor in Honduras, spent her spring break living with a poor family in the mountains of Honduras, sleeping on a dirt floor, living without electricity or running water. In the evenings she sat with the family in the twilight, singing, listening to stories around the fire. In that family, the elders were cherished, the children were adored. "That family," she said later, "made me think of my family. Compared with that family in Honduras, my family is dysfunctional. Why is it that we have so much, yet have so little of what matters?"

She went to Honduras to help the poor and surprise! She got helped. She went there rich, she returned poor. Which is good news because Jesus says, nobody who's rich and big can get into his kingdom. But then this good news: With God even the impossible is possible. Or is that bad news? [contextual]

You make the call.

As Athol Gill sums it up in *Life on the Road:*

> This is the only time in the gospels that we are specifically told of a person declining the call of Jesus—and, let the Western church mark and understand, he does so because of his material possessions! The young man who had such great potential disappears with the stage and we hear nothing more about him. Even his name has been forgotten.

C.S. Lewis once noted, "Now all things are possible. All things are possible. It is even possible to get a large camel through the small eye of a needle. That's possible. *But it will be extremely hard on the camel.*" [textual]

4 | The Use of Wonder in Sermon Development

HERE'S A BIT OF delicious irony to get us started. We want to be creative in our preaching to inspire our people to hear and obey the gospel. What happens if we're as boring as watching paint dry? Their minds drift elsewhere. Arthur Fry was an engineer in the paper products division of 3M. One Sunday morning in 1974, as he was sitting through a rather boring sermon, he conceived the idea of what we now know as the Post-it note.[1] I doubt his pastor sued for copyright infringement even though his boring sermon was an integral part of Fry's creative process. Even though I have nothing against adhesive pieces of note paper, I think we can inspire our people to do better. Don't you?

As was the case in the more theoretical chapters above, we can assume that many of the reasons for the use of wonder as well as its limitations are similar to those of wit. Even though they are not synonymous, wit and wonder do have a lot in common. At any rate, this should shorten the amount of content you will have to ingest during this chapter. In the course of these next pages, we will explore some of the ways wonder can be harnessed for the purposes of your preaching ministry. To this point we have been assuming that "wonder" expresses what most people mean by both "imagination" and "creativity." Even though we recognize that some

---

1. Jonah Lehrer, *Imagine*, 46–48.

The Use of Wonder in Sermon Development

treat imagination and creativity as synonyms, we have come to understand the former as the enhanced faculty of perceiving and the latter as the complementary faculty of conceiving. It will be helpful for our purposes from this point to distinguish between the two.

For those of you who still aren't sure whether this is a proper pursuit for a godly preacher, listen to the challenge offered by Eugene Peterson:

> Right now, one of the essential Christian ministries in and to our ruined world is the recovery and exercise of the imagination. Ages of faith have always been ages rich in imagination. It is easy to see why: the materiality of the gospel (the seen, heard and touched Jesus) is no less impressive than its spirituality (faith, hope, and love). Imagination is the mental tool we have for connecting material and spiritual, visible and invisible, earth and heaven.[2]

THE FUNCTIONS OF IMAGINATION

Imagination is a way of perceiving or of seeing. It includes the normal sense of sight but enhances it to the degree that we can we "see" what is below the surface, what others cannot see with the naked eye, what may be possible but isn't here yet. This faculty doesn't have to compete with rational or logical description but can complement it. If we over-emphasize one over the other, we become imbalanced. All logical description and we lose our humanity. All imagination and we lose touch with reality. So this is not a matter of either/or but both/and. A healthy person needs to be able to function in both these domains. This is not as easy as we might think, however. There are normal prejudices on both sides. Creative people look at logical thinkers and consider them pedantic and boring. Logical thinkers look at the creative types and think they're helpless dreamers because they see what isn't there—which to left-brained types seems senseless and even dishonest (maybe this is why Pablo Picasso says "Art is a lie that makes us all realize truth"). Most of

---

2. Eugene Peterson, *Under the Unpredictable Plant*, 171.

those in our culture have been more biased toward the left-brained, logical side of things for the most part. So we're simply trying to get matters back into balance a bit by developing the right-brained, intuitive and creative side. Here's what imagination can do for you:

Imagination Observes

The various forms of "seeing" build upon the physical sense of sight. Whether we are trained to be observant, as police officers are, or are just navigating our way through a normal day complete with routine tasks, we are employing the sense of sight. All sighted people share this in common. It is important to know that imagination is not some special gift that bypasses the normal capacity to see, but rather enhances it. This gives hope to all of us that our abilities to imagine can increase. This is not to say, by the way, that those without sight have no chance to be imaginative. We all know that not to be true. Physical sight is the *usual* foundation of imagination but not the essential one.

Imagination Focuses.

All of us who are able to observe, also know something else. There is a difference between "seeing" something and "noticing" it. We see countless things in a given day but only take notice of a few things (I learned this by asking my children what they learned in school today). This is not unhealthy, but necessary. If we paid close attention to everything we saw in a day, we would be candidates for a rubber room. Focusing on everything is out of the question. So then we must decide what to focus upon and why. If you have seen a close up photograph of a wild rose, you notice the fine detail of the flower in the foreground and that everything else seems a little blurry and out-of-focus. That's on purpose. We wouldn't notice the breath-taking beauty of the rose if everything else around it was vying for our attention. Our sense of sight works that way too. Normally we see what we want to see—in other words, we take notice of what interests us. If we buy something new, we begin to notice how many others have that same thing.

Imagination is not the only kind of observation that narrows its focus. Scientific forms of observation also value being able to notice and study objects with special care and detail. The major difference comes in the purpose of this penetrating attention. Most scientific observation is for the purposes of understanding and mastering the objects under investigation. Even if this mastery leads to the creation of something new, this new product is designed for some practical purpose. We imagine for the sheer joy and wonder it generates for us and for those who experience it with us. That's it. Granted, there might be by-products generated by the use of our imagination. People might want to pay us buckets of money just to share in our discovery, but that cannot be the ultimate reason we use our imagination. To create for the sole purpose of getting rich and famous is artistic prostitution.

Imagination Describes

Imagination calls us to put our observations into words. Imaginative thoughts can only be communicated if we wrestle them into the form of words. Otherwise they vanish into thin air. If we are noticing something, we need to leave a paper trail—a list of what we have noticed. Here is where we try to look from many different angles to see as much as we can. Much of imagination is simply taking the time to describe what we see from different perspectives. We will surprise ourselves with our level of imaginative thought if we are able to discipline ourselves in the practice of creative description. This ability will not develop overnight. It requires slow and dogged progress.

You could start with something as simple as describing an ordinary lead pencil. Start with merely ten descriptive statements about the pencil. Each time you return to this exercise, increase the number of descriptive statements by ten. Before long you will be able to come up with at least a hundred of these—and that is just about a pencil!

Imagination Resonates

Imagination is in the eye of the beholder. It involves the one doing the imagining. That is foundational. That is why imagination differs from logical description. Logic assumes a certain objectivity on the part of the one doing the observing (some even assume complete objectivity is possible and that the viewer can describe things as they are without any personal involvement). Imagination invites the viewer to be an integral part of the process. The process of imagining requires the observer to serve as some kind of central data depot. A lot of these impressions, memories, ideas and other data are lodged in the subconscious but it's all there. All this resonates within us to some degree of consciousness and our imagination produces results when connections are made between disparate bits of these data or impressions. That is why the imaginative idea that leads to a creative act or artifact bears the mark of its creator. We are the cauldron in which all this is brewing. That is why the process of creativity is more like a crock pot than a microwave oven.

Imagination Synthesizes

The power of imagination is in the connections made between ideas or impressions that go beyond the conventional or the expected. The power of logical analysis is in taking things apart to see how they work or might work better. In contrast, imagination seeks to make connections and to put things together. Imagination is the ability to think in several directions at once and see the connections between them. Surprising intersections may bubble to the surface. We may have seen note pads on one occasion and glue on another, but under the right conditions (like a boring sermon), we could come up with Post-it notes! It's as simple and complex as that. The longer all this bubbles inside of us, more connections are possible. There is no way to regulate this process. Sometimes it just keeps flowing out of you and other times there can be a long drought. The important discipline is to keep adding ideas and impressions to the pot. Then surprising things happen. We might find ourselves describing Baal the Canaanite fertility god and his female goddess

The Use of Wonder in Sermon Development

consort Asherah as Uncle and Antichrist (some ideas are more imaginative than others!).

Imagination Concretizes

Abstraction is the nemesis of imagination. An imaginative person is not one who is a captive to the world of ideas and ideals, dreams and disembodied visions. True imagination must be able to hit the ground. It is sensate, concrete and particular. As a matter of fact, homiletician (homileticians are scholars who teach preachers) Paul Scott Wilson states, "Excessive abstraction can be a sign of imagination that is stifled."[3] Imagination has no power in thin air. People cannot imagine anything if they have no concrete experience to serve as a launching pad.

Imagination Innovates

Here is where creativity comes in. Creativity takes the imaginative impression and turns it into something that we have not sensed before. It takes us beyond the normal or expected and breaks new ground. Part of our normal response to something creative is "That's really amazing but I think I could have come up with it myself when I think about it now." The point is, we didn't and someone else did. Innovation is not something completely new, but a creative variation on what we already know.

Imagination Synergizes

Most of us consider the imaginative person to be somewhat of a loner or recluse, a solitary visionary. That may be true of some, but doesn't do justice to all the facts. Imagination is contagious. There is something invigorating about being in an imaginative community, bouncing ideas off one another and giving birth to a creative environment. Jonah Lehrer points out, "The most creative ideas, it

---

3. Paul Scott Wilson, "Imagination," 268.

turns out, don't occur when we're alone. Rather, they emerge for our social circles, from collections of acquaintances who inspire novel thoughts."[4] Here preachers can learn from other creative vocations who spend time working together in teams. Larger churches already employ preaching teams and smaller ones can find ways of getting people together to form an imaginative community or creative team.

Imagination Inspires

We can be convinced by logic but we are moved by imagination. There is something about seeing a new possibility that engages us in a way that little else can. Our gaze is taken from what we know now as the normal and the expected and is transported to a world of new possibilities. Not all imaginative notions are of the same caliber. Some are as small as deft phrasing that temporarily lifts our spirits. Some may be as significant as the world-shaping words of Martin Luther King Jr.'s "I Have a Dream" speech. History looks back. Science looks around. Imagination looks ahead.

THE TYPES OF IMAGINATION

Conventional Imagination

This first type of imagination almost seems unimaginative in the way we have been using the term. This kind of imaginative capacity recognizes the importance and the power of the existing world of values, meaning, symbols and practices within the congregation. Preachers need to understand they enter a congregation that already has a collective imagination. No preacher starts from scratch. The preacher who ignores the existing ethos and imagination of the congregation will seldom be trusted enough to paint an alternative picture. To join and inhabit this way of viewing the world is the first step in stretching both preacher and congregation to dream new dreams and imagine a different world (or to imagine the world

---

4. Jonah Lehrer, *Imagine*, 204.

differently). Homiletician Thomas Troeger notes that "[e]ffective preachers honor the conventional imagination of the people to whom they preach because they realize it is the congregation's imaged/imagined world of holy meaning."[5] One practical result of this kind of imagination is it allows the preacher to predict the questions and objections forming the minds of members of the congregation so they might be answered in the course of the sermon.

Ethical (or communal) Imagination

This kind of imagination (which Fred Craddock and Thomas Troeger call "empathetic imagination") calls both preacher and congregation to the supreme ends of loving God and neighbor. We can imagine a world where we give of ourselves to God and each other so that our own desires and appetites are limited by the presence of the Other and others. This means nurturing a capacity to empathize with the needs of those around us, and drawing attention to situations where individualism and self-obsession threaten to destroy the depth and breadth of our salvation.[6]

Prophetic Imagination

The prophetic imagination (termed "visionary imagination" by Troeger)

> discerns the discrepancy between God's intention for the world, as revealed in scripture, and the world as it actually is. Prophetic imagination has a delimiting function, refusing to accept the limits the world holds as absolute or the limits we would place on God's power, seeking the possible in the impossible and the actual, the new in the old, the breaking in of God's realm in the midst of the mundane.[7]

---

5. Thomas Troeger, "Imagination/Creativity," 192.
6. Paul Scott Wilson, "Imagination," 267.
7. Ibid.

For too long we have viewed the prophets as angry rather than imaginative, condemning rather than creative. This hardly captures the heart of prophetic ministry. Prophets weave scenarios of both judgment and salvation. They picture what life will be like for God's people if they continue to forsake the covenant and experience the curses that follow. They also picture life as it should and will be when God restores the fortunes of those who return to the covenant and experience its blessings. Walter Brueggemann reminds us: "The task of prophetic ministry is to nurture, nourish, and evoke a consciousness and perception alternative to the consciousness and perception of the dominant culture around us."[8]

Poetic Imagination

This final form of imagination relates primarily to the use of language. It is ". . . the bringing into relationship of two ideas that normally would not be connected. In doing this, a spark of new meaning is produced."[9] This is part of what makes our language sparkle. The playful, somewhat unexpected juxtaposition of two different ideas engages the mind and fires the imagination of the congregation.

TEXTUAL USES OF IMAGINATION

As in the case with wit, wonder can be understood in relation to the biblical text itself, the person of the preacher and the context in which the imagination is employed.[10] The first of these is related to the biblical text. The preacher's use of imagination on the biblical text can be seen in several descending levels, starting with the structure and message of the entire book of the Bible from which

---

8. Walter Brueggemann, *The Prophetic Imagination*, 13.

9. Wilson, "Imagination," 267. Cf. also Paul Scott Wilson, *Imagination of the Heart*, 32–37.

10. For a discussion how this trialogue is to be understood broadly in terms of the entire preaching event, cf. Blayne A. Banting, *Take Up and Preach: A Primer for Interpreting Preaching Texts*, 26–38.

The Use of Wonder in Sermon Development

the preaching text is taken, down to the particular pericope to be preached and then to the very words and images found within the pericope.

The preacher needs to look at the occasion and message of each of the books of the Bible, to the extent that these can be determined, as an imaginative interpretive context for the sermon itself. If the congregation feels there is no way they could be impacted by the message of such ancient texts, it is the preacher's task to show fresh and relevant they can be. To begin with the kind of introduction to a book in the Bible like is done in the commentaries will almost certainly elicit yawns and encourage day-dreaming of the wrong sort. However, if we can make the connection between the first readers of the text and ourselves, the cobwebs and dust vanish and we get ready to hear an inspiring word. Can we inhabit a space similar to these ancient audiences? We can with a little bit of sanctified imagination. 1 Peter is a letter written to Christians who are wondering how they might live in the midst of a hostile host culture. Sound familiar? Malachi is written to people for whom life has flattened out and their expectations of God's provision have not been realized. 1 Corinthians speaks to believers who are having trouble leaving behind the baggage from their former way of life. All of this assumes that the Bible still addresses the issues that are most important to us as God's people. Our deepest needs have not changed over the past centuries, even though so many other things have. This use of imagination serves the truth of what Scripture claims for itself: "All Scripture is breathed out by God and profitable for teaching, for reproof, for correction, and for training in righteousness" (2 Tim 3:16).

The use of imagination in the preaching text itself is some of the most demanding work the preacher does. There is so much going on behind and within each text. The preacher is to ponder all this enough to get insights into how this text might be preached to a particular congregation at a particular place and time. There is a story behind every text and it is up to the preacher to be open to what that story might tell us about the text—to turn this ink back into blood and let it live. Train your eyes to watch for the back story behind every text.

With Wit and Wonder

There are proper exegetical procedures to follow and they should not be omitted or belittled. However, both hemispheres of the brain need to be engaged to get a living sense of the text. The ancient practice of *lectio divina* may help you with this. This slower, contemplative approach to the reading of the scriptural text can help you slow down and listen to what God may be saying to you in the text that you might miss with a more historical-grammatical reading. This kind of reading includes *lectio* (reading the text), *meditatio* (meditating on the text), *oratio* (praying the text), and *contemplation* (living the text). Eugene Peterson explains:

> Reading (*lectio*) is a linear act, but spiritual (*divina*) is not—any of the elements may be at the fore at any one time. There is a certain natural progression from one to the other, but after separating them in order to understand them we find that in actual practice they are not four discrete items that we engage in one after another in stair-step fashion. Rather than linear the process is more like a looping spiral in which all four elements are repeated, but in various sequences and configurations.... Each of the elements must be taken seriously; none of the elements may be eliminated; none of the elements can be practiced in isolation from the others. In the actual practice of *lectio divina* the four elements fuse, interpenetrate. *Lectio divina* is a way of reading that becomes a way of living.[11]

A more direct way to a deeper, more imaginative reading of the preaching text is to pepper it with all kinds of inquisitive questions. This reminds us that the text may have an overarching message, but has no unimportant parts. Details some might find unnecessary, such as sensate questions about the sights, sounds, tastes, smells and physical sensations in and around the text, are important to tease out. A helpful example has been supplied by Paul Scott Wilson in relation to the story of Zacchaeus (Luke 19:1–10). What is helpful is not the actual choice of question, because that must change with each text, but rather the thorough and imaginative way these questions might allow us to "get into the text."

11. Eugene Peterson, *Eat This Book*, 91.

The Use of Wonder in Sermon Development

-What was special about Jericho as a city?

-What kind of day was it? What time? What season?

-What indicates Zacchaeus was rich?

-Did his clothes make him stand out from the rest?

-Why was there a crowd? Had it gathered for Jesus? Why?

-Even if Zacchaeus were short, why could he not see Jesus?

-Wouldn't the crowd let him through?

-Did they not tolerate him?

-If the crowd was pressing tightly around Jesus, why did it do that?

-Why did Zacchaeus want to see Jesus?

-Was it not unusual for a wealthy man to climb a tree?

-Did Jesus know Zacchaeus before? Is that why he calls him by name?

-Is this another instance of Jesus just knowing the stranger's name?

-Did he ask someone?

-Or were some jeering Zacchaeus and shouting his name?

-Might that be why Jesus picked him?

-Why did Zacchaeus repent?

-Did Jesus demand this? Or was it a free response to being recognized?

-Did Jesus give him stature that the job and the tree could not?

-Do I like the story? Who do I like? What do I dislike?

-When have I been like Zacchaeus? The Crowd? Jesus?[12]

What remains is the imaginative use of the words and images in the preaching text. Many of the individual words in the text, especially the descriptive and theologically significant ones,

12. Wilson, *Imagination of the Heart*, 64, 65.

are connected to some kind of picture, symbol or image to begin with. It is the preacher's task to note these. Images are, by nature, evocative and so a great deal of the imaginative power of a sermon comes from paying attention to these images found right within the text itself. The preacher knows that "showing" is more powerful than "telling." With proper attention, texts begin to turn into picture galleries rather than buckets of words. We don't have to worry ourselves with the need to invent creative word pictures in order to communicate the preaching text. Often the most powerful ones are found right within the text. Fred Craddock reminds us that "[t]he place to begin discussing the function of imagination in preaching is not at the point of using imaginative words and phrases, but at the necessary prior point of receiving images."[13] If we are not in the habit of "seeing" these images in the preaching text, Warren Wiersbe has done us the great favor of highlighting many of the major images found in the Bible in his book *Preaching and Teaching with Imagination*.[14] He reminds us that, "[w]e have forgotten that the Bible is an imaginative book."[15]

PERSONAL USES OF IMAGINATION

If preaching is the communication of truth through personality as Phillips Brooks contends, then every preacher can and should be a uniquely creative communicator. None of us is a clone of another. Part of the preaching event is the unique relationship between the biblical text, the personality of the preacher, and the composition of the congregation. Each preacher, then, brings something different to this trialogue.

Personal Qualities

Each preacher is an endless combination of creative possibilities due in part to the particularities of identity. There is not another

13. Fred Craddock, *As One Without Authority*, 80.
14. Warren Wiersbe, *Preaching and Teaching with Imagination*, 89–198.
15. Wiersbe, "Imagination," 563.

The Use of Wonder in Sermon Development

soul under heaven who has been born when you were, to whom, when and where, with the gifts granted to you by God. Use all of these endowments to express your own particular imaginative slant to your preaching ministry. There is no room here to look over your shoulder at others with different experiences and giftings. You need to work with what you have been given and not waste valuable time pining for the life of someone else. If you're male or female, introverted or extraverted, athletic, musical, expressive or reserved, academic or pragmatic, tall or untall, thin or unthin, young or unyoung, take note of these qualities and employ them. Don't bemoan them but celebrate them. They form your creative slant—and that is as unique as your finger prints. Grant Howard points out: "Other human beings also have skills, even some of the same ones you have, but each person packages and delivers these skills in and through unique individualities. You are a custom-made person."[16] You don't have to have been on many world-wide travelling adventures, or have a dramatic conversion story, or have an exceptional gift with language to be creative. Often an attention to the smaller details of life can be the stuff of creative communication. Very few imaginative types have actually been to the moon—they simply have the capacity to make us think they have a summer cottage there.

Take advantage of the various personality assessment instruments out there if you lack self-knowledge in these areas. Ask others around you. There are creativity assessment instruments available as well, if you want to be that serious about determining the raw materials you have been given to determine your creativity quotient. Both here and in the following area of personal experiences, there is a delicate balance between knowing who you are and what you've done and not being too pre-occupied with yourself. Imagination is not a cover for narcissism.

Personal Experiences

Part of who you are is what you have done and what has been done to you. Again, you are unique in this regard. You will find it

---

16. Grant Howard, *Creativity in Preaching*, 62.

immensely helpful to have a working knowledge of your own autobiography. I'm not suggesting you write a book or a series of books highlighting your exploits (can you imagine me yawning right now?). Just know what you have done in enough detail that you can martial it in developing an imaginative perspective as well as giving you enough material to use in bringing life and light to the points you make in your preaching. Ask parents and relatives about your birth and early years. Recall or find out about your life at home. Where did you live? Who lived with you? What were your school years like? What vacations did you take—those you took alone or with family or friends? Who were your friends? Who were your enemies? What have you done for employment? What are some of the memorable events and stories from your past?

Don't stay in the past either. Your present also has great impact on your capacity to be imaginative. Who are you now? You might be an experienced preacher with a spouse and three grown children, working in an established congregation. You might be young and single or young with a young family and just getting underway in ministry. All this affects your imaginative slant. Use what God has given you, past and present, to communicate creatively.

Personal Disciplines

There are a few key disciplines that will help you become more imaginative in your sermon development.

First, do your homework. There is no shortcut to being imaginative. If you want to develop your imagination, you need to feed it with constant stimulation and regular discipline. Imaginative ideas are not birthed by immaculate conception, despite what you might have heard. Dedicate yourself to reading—read constantly, read widely, read alertly—fill your mind with the creative raw materials it needs to make imaginative connections and creations. Practice the art of creative description—employ your five senses in these descriptions. Write them down and then re-write them until you feel you've done it well. We've all heard that Mark Twain said "The difference between the right word and the nearly right word is the same as that between lightning and the lightning bug." Let your images be as real, concrete, vivid, succinct and evocative as possible. Keep practicing this craft. Attend to how you will transition in and out of this material and to when and where you will use it in your sermons. It is a long term commitment to hone your imaginative skills. Imaginative expositor Calvin Miller suggests, "[t]he creative spirit is nurtured by time and evaluation."[17]

Second, pay attention. Much of what you can use imaginatively comes from the mundane stuff of life. Loads of creative material floats, drives, walks, blows, gallops, slithers and trudges by us each day. What remains is for us to see it, notice it, and store it away for future use. You can train yourself to be more observant by taking time to notice. Practice people-watching. Sit down on a bench in the middle of the mall and watch what happens around you. If you're travelling, watch the sky, watch the terrain, watch the road signs and billboards, and if you're the one driving—watch the road! If you think your surroundings are boring, then you aren't looking hard enough.

Third, take your time. Imagination cannot be forced. We already have talked about this. Don't try to rush your imagination because most often it will freeze up on you. True creativity requires "simmering" time and does not respond to harried deadlines. This means you will need to take enough time to get away completely from what you are trying to create so your subconscious mind has time to do its work.

Fourth, take a chance. We probably are robbed of some very imaginative communication because the communicator didn't have the nerve to give it a shot. That doesn't mean every creative idea should be expressed. Some should be shelved, some should be hermetically sealed and dumped into the depths of the ocean. But on the whole, we are much the poorer because many creative ideas seem too "out there" to risk expressing. There is something about the very process of thinking sideways that requires a certain amount of audacity simply because imagination takes us where no-one has gone before. Our imagination sees connections and

---

17. Calvin Miller, *Preaching*, 227.

perspectives others do not. It does take a certain amount of nerve to express the previously un-expressed. We risk all kinds of ridicule and misunderstanding. The imaginative person needs a bit of what the Yiddish call *chutzpah* or audacity. Jonah Lehrer notes: "The reason chutzpah is so important has to do with the nature of new ideas, which are inherently precarious."[18] The fact there is no money back guarantee that a given new or creative idea will "make it" means we need to be willing to take some measure of risk.

CONTEXTUAL USES OF IMAGINATION

The preacher cannot ignore the third party in the trialogue between text, preacher and congregation. When a preacher's imagination miss-fires, often it is due to a misreading of the congregation's capacity to understand and appreciate what or how the preacher has spoken. This necessary part of creative communication means the preacher should be paying attention to those who receive the sermons as much as to the raw materials from which imagination comes. Get to know the demographics of your congregation. Understand the age, gender, socio-economic, political and educational composition of those who hear you preaching every week. Recognize the difference that time and place make to how you express your imagination. Is this the regular Sunday morning worship service or a retreat setting? What about time of day? What about the occasion? Is this during Lent? Is this a wedding or a funeral? What is the mood of the congregation—open, boisterous, solemn? What is their history? Have they shown aptitude for appreciating imagination in the past? What are their sacred cows? How are you, as the preacher, received by the congregation—are you walking on thin ice or can you walk on water?

All these factors come into play in how you are able to develop your sermon in an imaginative way. Understood and used wisely, these may make the difference between a good or passable sermon

---

18. Jonah Lehrer, *Imagine*, 242.

The Use of Wonder in Sermon Development

and a great one. Warren Wiersbe reminds us: "Imagination is what transforms a craftsman into an artist."[19]

As we did in the previous chapter, we conclude with a sample sermon. This time, however, we'll take the plunge and look at a sermon preached by the author in his own congregational setting. This is not included because it is the epitome of imagination. Far from it—it is a sermon that comes out of regular congregational life with all its time pressures and weekly rhythms. We had been working through the epistle of 1 Peter for several weeks and landed on 1 Peter 2:11–3:12 for the Sunday of Mothers' Day 2010. So much for the benefits of sermon planning! The fact that this text deals with the issue of submission and having to preach it on such an occasion made me wonder if I might try something out of the ordinary to address this strange situation. Part of what I was at pains to do was to show the wider context of the issue of submission so we would not try to hijack the issue through our contemporary biases that highlight the husband-wife relationship and ignore the others.

Although I seldom do this as a matter of course, I decided to preach this sermon as a first person narrative complete with time period costuming. There were some considerable challenges to this approach. This is not a narrative text and so I would have to construct the back story so the congregation could identify with the narration of the sermon. This required piecing together some of the biblical background known about Peter and a little bit of poetic license in giving a plot conflict to this story. I tried to do this by keying in on Peter's difficulty with submitting to others (not too hard to see from some of his actions) and to his mother-in-law (not found in the text but is a common theme in our present culture). This meant a fair bit of creative thought (and license) being exercised before one word of the sermon was written. Our congregation isn't used to this form of preaching, nor was I used to delivering it this way, but it seemed like a risk worth taking on this particular occasion. For what it's worth, I haven't preached another first person narrative sermon since! Again I will give interpretive comments

---

19. Warren Wiersbe, "Imagination," 565.

through bold bracketed statements and identify textual, personal and contextual aspects of imagination.

Submission Impossible [word play on Mission Impossible]

Beloved, I urge you as sojourners and exiles to abstain from the passions of the flesh, which wage war against your soul. Keep your conduct among the Gentiles honorable, so that when they speak against you as evildoers, they may see your good deeds and glorify God on the day of visitation.

Be subject for the Lord's sake to every human institution, whether it be to the emperor as supreme, or to governors as sent by him to punish those who do evil and to praise those who do good. For this is the will of God, that by doing good you should put to silence the ignorance of foolish people. Live as people who are free, not using your freedom as a cover-up for evil, but living as servants of God. Honor everyone. Love the brotherhood. Fear God. Honor the emperor.

Servants, be subject to your masters with all respect, not only to the good and gentle but also to the unjust. For this is a gracious thing, when, mindful of God, one endures sorrows while suffering unjustly. For what credit is it if, when you sin and are beaten for it, you endure? But if when you do good and suffer for it you endure, this is a gracious thing in the sight of God. For to this you have been called, because Christ also suffered for you, leaving you an example, so that you might follow in his steps. He committed no sin, neither was deceit found in his mouth. When he was reviled, he did not revile in return; when he suffered, he did not threaten, but continued entrusting himself to him who judges justly. He himself bore our sins in his body on the tree, that we might die to sin and live to righteousness. By his wounds you have been healed. For you were straying like sheep, but have now returned to the Shepherd and Overseer of your souls.

Likewise, wives, be subject to your own husbands, so that even if some do not obey the word, they may be won without a word by the conduct of their wives, when they see your respectful and pure conduct. Do not let your adorning be external—the braiding of hair and the putting on of gold jewelry, or the clothing you wear— but let your adorning be the hidden person of the heart with the imperishable beauty of a gentle and quiet spirit, which in God's sight is very precious. For this is how the holy women who hoped in God used to adorn themselves, by submitting to their own husbands, as Sarah obeyed Abraham, calling him lord. And you are her children, if you do good and do not fear anything that is frightening.

Likewise, husbands, live with your wives in an understanding way, showing honor to the woman as the weaker vessel, since they are heirs with you of the grace of life, so that your prayers may not be hindered.

Finally, all of you, have unity of mind, sympathy, brotherly love, a tender heart, and a humble mind. Do not repay evil for evil or reviling for reviling, but on the contrary, bless, for to this you were called, that you may obtain a blessing. For

"Whoever desires to love life
and see good days,
let him keep his tongue from evil
and his lips from speaking deceit;
let him turn away from evil and do good;
let him seek peace and pursue it.
For the eyes of the Lord are on the righteous,
and his ears are open to their prayer.
But the face of the Lord is against those who do evil." (1 Peter 2:11–3:12)

Shalom. My name is Shimon ben Johanan. You might not recognize my name but that's all right because Jesus changed it anyway. He didn't think it suited me. Shimon means "one who hears." For some reason he thought I needed another name. My mother-in-law agreed with Jesus: "He's always talking—so how can he be listening?" So Jesus called me Cephas which means "rock." You probably know me best as Peter which means "rock" in your language. My mother-in-law looked at my head and said, "That's more like it!" That's my mother-in-law! [**contextual**]

With Wit and Wonder

You may have read where my good friends Mark and Luke tell the story of how Jesus healed my mother-in-law once when she was sick with a fever. They don't tell us why she was sick. What I didn't tell them was who spiked her soup with the spoiled fish! You know what they say—a bad fish a day keeps the mother-in-law away! "He's always talking—how can he be hearing?"—my eye! **[some poetic license to set up the story of how Peter has struggled with submission—contextual and textual]**

I'm going to talk to you today about submission. You might have guessed already that I've had some problems with submission in my life—and not just with my mother-in-law. When I first started following Jesus, I stood aside for no-one. I was large and in charge, I spoke my mind. I was always first to volunteer. I was first to draw my sword. I was always the first to speak. Maybe Shimon wasn't such a good name for me after all.

I had this issue with submission but I wasn't the only one with issues when we first started following Jesus. My fishing buddy John had this terrible temper. When he got mad, he could scare fish right into the boat! **[more poetic license]** Jesus even gave him a nickname—he called him one of the sons of thunder. We all laughed about that! That's John—no lightning, just thunder—all yap and no zap! After he spent time with Jesus, you know him as the Apostle of Love. Quite a turn-around! And Thomas had this problem with doubt. He always had to see it for himself. He ended up dying for his faith in India. There is no doubt about that! And then there was Judas Iscariot. He had this issue with backstabbing—well I guess even Jesus didn't bat a thousand! **[a bit of levity—textual]** So I had to learn to deal with my pride and my unwillingness to submit.

It seems like you people have issues with submission too. This week your preacher comes to me—all nervous and edgy—worried about having to preach on submission on Mothers Day. He was even trying to get people to sneeze on him so he could call in sick. **[a bit of banter to draw attention to the undue emphasis we place on the difficulty of this issue]** He sounds like a bit of a "scaredy pants" to me. **[some self-deprecating humour]** So he says to me, "You wrote this stuff, *you* preach it!" So I will. **[personal]**

The Use of Wonder in Sermon Development

There are a couple things I don't understand. Of all the relationships I talk about in this text, the one you have the most trouble with is the one between husbands and wives. That was least on the list for my first readers. They were in danger from nasty leaders, from their task masters and from most of the society in general. If you don't believe me, ask some of your own missionaries in that part of the world today. If all you worry about is getting along with your spouse—you should be so lucky! [**putting the situation into perspective—contextual**]

Here's the other thing: why do you mistake an unnatural thing for an unwanted thing? Submitting to others isn't natural—I know that as well as anyone. That doesn't mean it's bad, it just needs to be learned. The truth is that submission is central to living the Christian life. [**main sermon focus or theme**] If you're having trouble with submitting it might be that you have been hoodwinked by the western intellectual tradition of the autonomous individual. You may think your identity is wrapped up in your ability to choose for yourself and to demand your own rights as a person. There are only three things wrong with that: it's wrong, it's pagan, and it doesn't work! [**contextual**]

My friend Paul knows what I'm talking about. He says our identity is found "in Christ" and that is something social before it's personal. It has to do with "we" before being "me." We are the most free when we are together "in Christ." So submission doesn't really limit our freedom, it expresses it! How could that be, you say? Submission is the willing and gracious bending of our will to another's not because we have to but because we want to. It's bending, not being bent. Submission is not giving up, or giving in. It is giving away. [**piling of statements designed for rhetorical effect—textual**] Submission can only be given, it cannot be taken. If you think you can demand submission from somebody else, you don't deserve it.

Now I think we're ready to hear what I say about submission in this text. [**the sermon is heavily front-loaded due to the subject matter—contextual**] Basically what I'm saying is that it's not about you, it's about the gospel. Look at 2:12: "Keep your conduct among the Gentiles honorable, so that when they speak against you as evildoers, they may see your good deeds and glorify God on the day of visitation." So what I want to know is, how can we act toward unbelieving rulers, slave masters, spouses and society in general so that we don't give the gospel a black eye?

Let's start with the political leaders. How can you support the goodness of the gospel when you are ruled by people who don't care about the gospel or you or anything but themselves? I give the key in verse 16: "Live as people who are free, not using your freedom as a cover-up for evil, but living as servants of God." We can live as free people but as free people we are still servants of God. He is the one with final authority here. These other leaders do have power and sometimes they can make our lives miserable, but that doesn't change the fact of who is ultimately in control. So where and when we are able, let's graciously submit to these unbelieving leaders for the sake of the gospel. Remember who was Emperor of Rome when I wrote this—it was this fiddle-playing fiend named Nero. [textual] Talk about a challenge! So part of our lives as believers is to submit to the governing authorities as long as they don't demand what God says we can't give them. We can still, most of the time, obey them graciously and submit to their authority as both free people and God's servants.

The next part may be a bit of a stretch for you because I talk about submitting to your masters. Your lives are not owned by someone else—no matter how much of a grind you're in. You might think you owe your soul to the company store. [contextual] Is it really that bad? Many of those first believers were owned body and soul by someone else. Lots of these masters were nasty too. Not all of them, but many were—especially when they felt our faith was un-Roman. This is often not a great place to be but we can still submit to them—for the sake of Christ and the gospel—even to the nasty ones.

Don't miss what I say next because this is where we get the power to do what doesn't come naturally to us. I put this right in the middle of the text because it's the most important part. Here is why we can take a licking and keep on ticking. [textual] Jesus travelled this road before all of us and suffered unjustly for us. When we are suffering, even when we're in the right, we can look to Jesus. He left us the example to follow. There is a lot about Jesus that we should

The Use of Wonder in Sermon Development

notice. I know—I was there with him for over three years. There are his teachings and his many miracles over nature, disease and demons. But notice I mention his sufferings here. This is what I want you to see. "He committed no sin, neither was deceit found in his mouth. When he was reviled, he did not revile in return; when he suffered, he did not threaten, but continued entrusting himself to him who judges justly. He himself bore our sins in his body on the tree, that we might die to sin and live to righteousness. By his wounds you have been healed. For you were straying like sheep, but have now returned to the Shepherd and Overseer of your souls."

Can you see him here? Hanging on the cross. Bruised and bleeding. The scent of death everywhere. [textual] He's leaving this example of selfless suffering in the face of injustice. He's the ultimate example of how to suffer this way. One of your own theologians—some guy named Helmut (and you think our names are weird!)—has said "Jesus is not our model, he is the prototype." [textual]

But there's more. Do you notice something familiar in what I say here? Do you hear the echoes from Isaiah chapter 53 here? Not only does Jesus give us the example of how to submit in the middle of injustice. He also bears ours sins for us by taking them to the cross with him so we might be free to die to our sin and live for his righteousness. Here's where the power to submit comes from. Jesus is so gracious to us, he doesn't just tell us to do something we can't do by ourselves. He also gives us the example to follow *and* the power to do what we couldn't do before. Remember, this submitting is not really about us at all. It's more about him. We could never do something this unnatural without his power.

Now we get to the part about husbands and wives. I tell believing wives to submit to their own husbands, even the unbelieving ones. Do you see a theme here? We are to submit to our leaders, even the unbelieving ones. We are to submit to our masters, even the nasty ones. Now wives are to submit to their husbands, even the unbelieving ones. Get it? When we are submitting, we are really submitting to God and so we don't need to stress over whether a person deserves our submission. But God does deserve it. Back in my day, if a wife became a believer without her husband's permission she was being insubordinate. So I say to wives, don't demand your rights as one who is free, but follow the example of Jesus. Allow your gracious and loving actions and your inner beauty to speak for themselves.

You husbands need to listen to me. You are bigger and stronger than your wives. Don't take advantage of that and demand respect and obedience from them. There is no room for bullies in God's kingdom. Treat your wives with respect and love. If you have to demand submission from them, you don't deserve it. So listen to her. Offer to do the dishes. Tell her how much you love her. Share the TV remote. Watch figure skating with her once in a while. [**contextual**]

From there I move on to how we are to live in the midst of a hostile culture—from what happens inside the house to what happens outside of it. You guys may think you have it tough here. You should have been back in my time! You have a lot of brothers and sisters around the world who understand this way more than you do. [**contextual**] Some of your English translations make it sound like I'm talking about how you are to treat each other in the church. That's not what I meant. I'm showing you how to live in the midst of those who don't like you and often mistreat you because of your trust in Jesus. So don't walk around with a holy chip on your shoulder, Don't return fire for fire, but instead bless the ones who mistreat you. Send flowers, not letter bombs. [**contextual**] You'll feel much better and they won't know what hit them! In this way you receive a blessing and become a blessing all at the same time.

So that's what I mean by submission. It's still unnatural, but it's not unhealthy. It's the sign of strength, not weakness. It's learning how to bend our will to others because we want to and not because we have to. Jesus died so we could actually do this and he even gave us the supreme example of how it's done.

So, now I'm learning how to submit. It hasn't been an easy road but it's been a healthy one. Now I'm not just taking—I'm learning to give. I'm not always demanding—now I'm receiving. And now I'm not always talking—now I'm learning to listen for the sake of Christ and a lost world. And my mother-in-law? Do you know what she calls me now? She calls me Shimon because now I hear. And that's a good thing. [**contextual**]

5 | Wit and Wonder in Sermon Delivery

YOU HAVE WADED THROUGH a mountain of material to get to this point. Congratulations! Now we get to the part that might either disappoint or encourage you, scare or excite you—the actual demonstration of some of the wit and wonder you might use in some of your own sermons. What follows is not intended to be copied (a lot of it isn't worth copying anyway). Wit and wonder are not for parroting but for producing your own in your own context. Do not be limited by the examples that follow but allow them to inspire you to use your own capacities of humour and imagination. There will be no direction in terms of the actual art of delivering the sermon itself. You will need to consult full length books that address those issues.[1]

USE A VIDEO CLIP

We might as well get to this right away. In our technological age, where image is king and we spend more of our time in front of screens of various sizes, it is very tempting to want to keep pace and communicate in a way people understand. Enter audio-visual technology. Few churches have no screen and video projection any

---

1. Cf. Jana Childers and Clayton J. Schmit, eds. *Performance in Preaching: Bringing the Sermon to Life*. Grand Rapids, MI: Baker, 2008.

more. This is the era in which we live. If we lag too far behind, we fear we will be written off as irrelevant. In one sense, video clips are just the newest version of the story which has long been accepted as helpful illustrative material for preaching. But before we completely jump on the digital bandwagon, there are some sobering warnings to heed.

The first of these warnings is the most important to the purposes of this book, since we're trying to become more creative, not less. Video clips can be used as a shortcut to using other, more labor-intensive creative devices. In this way, the imagination of the preacher is left untested in taking this easier road. If overused, video also leaves the imagination of the congregation unengaged because the video images do the work of imagination for them. Robert Howard warns, ". . .an over-reliance on visual imagery in the sermon can undercut its conceptual progression or simply produce the emotional catharsis of an entertained audience rather than significant growth toward faithful discipleship."[2] We don't want to turn the congregation into a passive audience. All corporate worship, including the sermon, is to engage the worshippers, not entertain them.

The second warning relates to all forms of technology (both low-tech and high-tech). Technology tends to take over unless we intentionally use it only toward higher ends. Quentin Schultze reminds us: "Presentational technologies should be fit to worship, not the other way around."[3] I have been present in worship services where the technology takes over and either turns worship into entertainment or the sermon into a boardroom presentation which over-dogmatizes the sermon and squeezes all the imagination out of both the sermon and the congregation.

The third and final warning is practical. If there is a preacher behind the pulpit and there is constant use of the screen—where does the congregation focus? Is that not a bit confusing? We need to be careful that we do not confuse the congregation by demanding they constantly switch back and forth between seeing a disembodied

2. Robert Howard, "Technology and the Sermon," 368.
3. Quentin Schultze, "Technology," 334.

Wit and Wonder in Sermon Delivery

image on the screen and listening to an embodied preacher on the platform. "A preacher embodie[s] God's speech."[4]

All this said, I have used video clips in my preaching. There are a couple of ways this might be done. You can use video clips from the many on-line sources that offer such services. Some of these are free and others require a subscription cost of some kind. You will need to give credit where credit is due when you use them, which is no different, really, than the ethics required in the use of any illustrative material not your own. The other option is to use clips from feature length movies. There are a few land mines here. Be careful not to use movie clips from movies that will traumatize or scandalize the congregation. This is not the time to impress the congregation with your panache as an *avante garde* film critic. Stick to what you don't have to apologize for afterwards. Marc Newman suggests the popular and outstanding older films are best.[5] There might be occasions when you are responding to some new film sensation that you bend these rules. Be careful, however, that your preaching ministry is just that and not a social commentary on what is fashionable at the moment. Personally I have used movie clips from a variety of movies, from *The Passion of the Christ* to *Dumb and Dumber*, but still use them sparingly.

Another option is to make your own video clips. Many churches have these capabilities given the wide accessibility of digital video equipment. This allows more creative expression as you are able to contextualize the content to the part of the sermon you want to illustrate. Such efforts are time consuming, and without a video production ministry within your congregation, you will need to give your video people ample time to produce these clips. For example, for a sermon on the armor of God from Ephesians 6:10–20, we shot a sports interview with myself in complete football gear as Jack "the Sack" Lombardi, the Lord's Linebacker. This short clip was a mixture of sports interview clichés and a comparison of the various pieces of football equipment with the armor of God. At least the football fans seemed engaged!

---

4. Ibid., 335.
5. Marc Newman, "Video Clips," 209.

With Wit and Wonder

I noted in chapter 1 that the flow of the redemptive story in Scripture could be pictured in the comedic shape with six different chapters. To introduce a six part sermon series on each of these chapters we shot a rap with me taking on the persona of B-Layne, a white, middle-aged rapper. Go ahead and laugh, it was supposed to be funny! These were the lyrics of the rap entitled "The Story:"

> We all need a story
> To show us how to live
> To tell us who we are—
> Our own metanarrative.
>
> The Bible tells God's story
> And we've a part to play
> It's the story of redemption:
> Creation to Judgment Day.
>
> The story is a long one
> It has six different parts
> It tells us about Yahweh
> Whose love is "off the charts."
>
> Chapter One is Creation
> When God created everything
> The whole world was as bright
> And shiny as my bling.
>
> Man and woman in the garden
> And everything was good
> All in perfect harmony
> The way God knew it could.
>
> Chapter Two is the Coup
> Mankind rebelled against God
> After all he did for them
> That seemed a little odd.
>
> The serpent was the tempter
> And was on the attack
> The ate forbidden fruit
> And the whole thing went WHACK!

Chapter Three is Covenants
God made Israel his own
With Land, law and a king
To sit on David's throne.

They were to light the way
But sin made their light go dim
They were taken into exile
It was "lights out" for them.

Chapter Four is the Christ
God sent his Son to save
Because all mankind was lost
And didn't believe or behave.

Jesus died for our sins
And rose to make us free
Salvation to all who believe
For them, you, and me.

Chapter Five is the Church
The body of God's own Son
People of every nation and tribe
Whose freedom Christ has won.

The church is on a mission
To make disciples of the lost
To spread the gospel near and far
No matter what the cost.

Chapter Six is Consummation
When God's plan is complete
A new heaven and earth begin
After Jesus' judgment seat.

Tears and death will be no more
And life will never end
All that's wrong will be made right
By Christ our Lord and Friend.

With Wit and Wonder

> This is redemption story
> Our present, future, and past
> It can show you the way
> To living that will last.
>
> This story of redemption
> Is our own story too
> God wants to have us in it
> So now how about you?

SING A SONG

Speaking of getting a bad rap, you also might try your hand at composing some music. You may feel way out of your comfort and competence zone here, but try it if you feel you might pull it off. If you have *bona fide* musical ability, you could try composing short songs that express the truth of your sermon. Don't let the song hijack the sermon but make it fit the sermon—we can tend to be carried away by own creative efforts, and this is particularly true of music. However, if you are lacking in the capacity to write music, you can use existing tunes and write your own lyrics. This has the advantage of well-known tunes that the congregation knows already.

For a sermon on the Song of the Vineyard from Isaiah 5:1–7, for a brief moment I became Isaiah Ben Amoz, a country and western singer (with cowboy hat and ukulele for comic effect) and sang the following song to the tune of Kenny Rogers' "*Lucille:*"

> You picked a fine time to leave me Judah,
> I made you a vineyard, and gave it to ya';
> I was lookin' for good grapes
> But you gave me wild ones;
> So I'll squeeze you until you whine.
> You picked a fine time to leave me Judah.

On another occasion, preaching on the calming of the storm in Mark 4:35–41, I started with my own version of this "fateful trip" by using the theme music from *Gilligan's Island*:

> So sit right back and you'll hear a tale

> A tale of a fateful trip
> That started from this holy port
> Aboard this tiny ship.
> The guys were mighty sailing men,
> The Savior brave and sure.
> Twelve passengers set sail that day
> For a three hour tour, a three hour tour.
> The weather started getting rough,
> The tiny ship was tossed
> If not for the presence of their sleeping Lord,
> Their lunches would be lost, their lunches would be lost. . . .

Just a brief note on what you might be wondering about the level of my maturity and/or sanity. Many of these examples are taken from over 35 years of preaching and so have been sprinkled between rather long bouts of sanity over a long period of time. I appreciate your concern—really, I do.

USE AN OBJECT

Intentionally go low-tech once in a while and bring something with you into the pulpit that illustrates the message of your sermon. Even in this high-tech era, concrete objects still have communicative power. Yes, that even means bringing a concrete cinder block, to those prone to puns! It is a mistake to save all the object lessons for the children's sermon—the adults in the congregation are paying more attention anyway!

In trying to preach on Jesus' teaching on divorce in the gospels, I wanted to highlight the fact that he referred back to the previous teaching on marriage in Genesis 2:24 on the two becoming one flesh. So I noted how Jesus' comments fit with the Bible's own philosophy of marriage. And who better to help us with our philosophy than Plato? At this point I brought out 2 cans of Play Doh—one blue and the other pink. I held up the blob of blue Play Doh and said "This is the husband." I then held up the blob of pink Play Doh in the other hand and said, "And this is the wife." Then I took the 2 lumps and squished them together until they were entirely mixed together and then said, "And this is marriage. Any questions?"

On another occasion, in giving some geographical background to a sermon on an Old Testament text, I used by own body as a map of ancient Palestine. The right side of your body serves as the western coastline of Palestine with your right shoulder being the location of Mt. Carmel. Your mouth serves as the Sea of Galilee, your nose as Mt. Hermon, and if you happen to be wearing a tie, it can be the Jordan River. You can use your own imagination from there, especially if you're wearing a Bible belt! Come up with your own ways to use objects to creatively get your word across.

USE A PARODY

You can use the congregation's knowledge of their culture to parody some of these things to help with your sermon. In order to do this well, you need to have a good comprehension of their cultural awareness. On a few different occasions, I have used a Top Ten list like the one on the Late Show with David Letterman to make my point. You can add items to the list that only make sense to your own congregation and context and this gives the congregation ownership of it and is more engaging anyway.

Parody is a form of satire and so not everyone will be able to follow your line of reasoning. Sometimes you risk being taken literally and that can sabotage your point. This was a lesson I learn several years ago when I watched in disgust to see Canadian Olympic snow-boarder Ross Rebagliati test positive for marijuana after he'd won the gold medal. The International Olympic Committee (IOC) was threatening to take away the medal and Rebagliati's only defense was that he must have inhaled second hand marijuana smoke. This seemed like a major black eye for the country and amateur sport generally. So I decided in protest that we would need new lyrics for the Canadian National Anthem when Rebagliati was standing on the middle podium:

> O Cannabis! Our home-grown native weed!
> True potent buzz that our snow boarders need!

> With glowing joints, they rack up the points,
> Our snowboarding team is hot!
> But, by and large, O Cannabis
> The sport has gone to pot!
> God, make each toke, give no secondhand smoke
> O Cannabis, we stand in need of thee!
> O Cannabis, PPHHFFT to the IOC!

My issue was that some did not get the satirical intent and felt I was lobbying for marijuana use! So you use such material at some risk.

TELL A STORY

There are many variations to this time-honored skill. Stories are powerful and because of this, take care they do not overpower your sermon. Stories reach out and capture people and so you need to guard that these "captives" are being lead toward the point of your sermon, not to some other destination of their own choosing. You might tell an anecdote from your own life like the story of the mauve sofa by John Ortberg in chapter 3. You might tell an anecdote from the experience of others (as long as you make it perfectly clear and don't try to claim it as your own). You might retell a story from history including stories from the Bible. These allow you to use your powers of imagination to help everyone feel like they are right on the scene of the story itself. Immerse yourself into the details of the story and use your senses to describe what you are experiencing. Practice this with the story of Jonah and the whale (speaking of immersing yourself!), or the fall of Jericho, or Elijah on Mt. Carmel. You might try some creative contemporizing of at least parts of these stories. The jolt of the juxtaposition of the ancient and the contemporary (like having the prophets of Baal dancing around their altar on top of Mt. Carmel singing *"Come on Baal, light my fire!"*) can engage the congregation in creative ways. You might try your hand at creating a fictional story—like Jesus' parables.

There are different ways to employ these stories in your sermons. Some will give direct and literal support to what you are trying to get across. Other stories may be used figuratively or analogically to give more indirect support to your point. You could tell the story and then note how it connects to what you have been saying. For example:

> To illustrate the value of persevering in prayer, we could tell a newspaper story of a man who proposed to a woman eight times over six years before she finally accepted. We might conclude, "In a similar way, prayer sometimes requires making repeated requests before it's answered."[6]

TAKE ON A CHARACTER

A variation on telling a story is to tell it from the first person. You might want to attempt period costuming or not, experiment with possible accents or simply use your own natural voice, stick to the actual details of the story or biblical narrative or use a little poetic license to add plot, characterization and dialogue to the story. You could tell it from the perspective of the protagonist in the story or the antagonist or one of the minor characters—your only limitations are your imagination and good taste. A word of warning, however, if you want to get a bit more theatrical with your telling of the story: make sure you indeed have the dramatic gifts or such an imaginative approach could be a disaster. Your calling is to be a faithful preacher, not an amateur actor, a theologian, not a thespian. There is nothing more pathetic than preachers who think they are actors when they're not.

USE AN IMAGE

Images are evocative by nature. You can unleash this power by using carefully and creatively crafted images in your preaching. You might project an actual image on the screen. I have done this in several different ways over the years, depending on the effect I was looking for. Some projected images elicit understanding, some awe and wonder, some comic relief. Know why you are using each image

---

6. Mark Galli and Craig Brian Larson, *Preaching That Connects*, 59.

and do not overload the sermon with so many that the sharpness of your message is blunted or diffused.

Verbal images are actually more powerful than visual ones since they deeply engage the imagination of those in the congregation. Images are closely related to metaphors, similes, analogies, and symbols. All of these have the capacity to engage the collective imagination of those hearing the sermon and drives your point home in a way that is deeper than pure intellectual assent. Note the sensate imagery in this paragraph from a sermon by Chuck Swindoll on Psalm 138:

> [David] says, "I will sing of it before the gods." . . . It's easy for us to forget that this little finger of land called Palestine was actually an island of monotheism surrounded by a sea of polytheism—paganism, heathendom—whose idols were numerous, and often obscene. . . . If you ever have the privilege of traveling in the Orient, you will see the gods visibly. You will see them on rooftops, and you will see them by door posts. You will see them stories high, covered with gold. You'll see their feet and legs as they sit like huge, fat giants, marked by blood and the droppings of candles. You'll smell the incense.[7]

USE POETRY

Poetry is creative by nature. It is also emotive by nature which means it needs to be used with wisdom. Poetry, read properly, requires slow smoldering contemplation. This doesn't always serve the purposes of the sermon, so you will need to use it wisely. Often a well-chosen few lines is preferable to longer quotations—just enough to make your point. You are there to preach and not offer an appreciative interpretation of the poem (just don't tell the poet I said that!). Song lyrics and hymn lyrics fall into this category as well. I long remember the impact of the final two lines of *When I Survey the Wondrous Cross*, spoken in timely fashion in a sermon I

---

7. In Galli and Larson, *Preaching That Connects*, 64, 65.

heard in my youth: "Love so amazing, so divine, Demands my soul, my life, my all."

If you are gifted poetically, you might try writing some of your own poetry. Again, do not use too much in a given sermon, but enough to give support to the message. Depending on your intent, you might alter the style of poetry. If it is wonder you want, use true poetry. If it is wit, bits of doggerel work best.

Another poetic device is the refrain. This terse and powerful phrase can be repeated at planned intervals in the sermon. I still remember the refrain, "That was Friday, but Sunday's comin'" from a sermon by Tony Campolo. The African-American preaching tradition is rich in this kind of rhetorical power. Immerse yourself in the creative sermons that are readily available these days.

That is probably sufficient to get your own creative juices flowing for the benefit of your own preaching ministry. Remember that predictability is your enemy and surprise and awe are your friends. Get to know your friends and leave predictability no forwarding address. May God bless you with all the wit and wonder you need to speak his Word to his people for his glory. Amen.

Appendix A
Forms of Humour (with examples from the Gospels)

A Fortiori: An argument from the lesser to the greater. Granting a certain fact about the lesser, it becomes even more compelling on the larger scale. Matthew 7:9–11; 10:25.

Caricature: A form of exaggerated imitation where the qualities of a person are targeted to produce a ridiculous effect. Matthew 6:2, 5, 16; 23:24.

Counter Question: A question asked in response to one asked by one's opponent in order to silence the opponent. Matthew 21:24, 25; 22:18, 19.

Hyperbole: Bold overstatement, or extravagant exaggeration of fact, either for serious or comic effect. Matthew 7:3; 23:24; Mark 10:25.

Invective: Direct denunciation (in contrast to the indirect approach of irony) by the use of derogatory descriptions. The use of invective is not to express personal hatred but commits the one using it and the one at whom it is aimed to a certain moral standard. Matthew 23:13–32; Luke 11:42–52.

Irony: A double-leveled literary phenomenon in which two tiers of meaning stand in some opposition to each other and in which some degree of unawareness is expressed or implied. The "punch" of irony depends in part upon someone

Appendix A

failing to see it. Local irony occurs at a given point in the text though its punch may depend upon knowledge gained by the reader elsewhere, either in the text or outside it. Luke 5:32; 13:33; 22:36; 24:18; Mark 7:9; John 2:19.

Meiosis: A deliberate understating of the importance of something or someone for effect. Luke 17:9.

Metaphor: An analogy identifying one object with another and ascribing to the to the first object one or more of the qualities of the second. Luke 13:32; Matthew 23:33.

Paradox: A statement that although seemingly contradictory or absurd may actually be well founded or true. Luke 9:60; 12:3; Matthew 5:5; 18:3, 4; 21:31; 23:11; Mark 8:35.

Parody: Where a weighty style is used in relation to more inconsequential subject matter. Matthew 16:2-4.

Proverb: A saying that briefly and memorably expresses some recognized truth about life. Matthew 5:14; Mark 6:4; Luke 4:23.

Pun: A play on words that are either identical in sound or very similar in sound, but are sharply different in meaning (very hard to detect in translated text). Matthew 16:18.

Rhetorical Question: A question for which there is a rather obvious answer but the speaker is more interested in increasing the rhetorical impact of his or her point than to induce the right answer. Matthew 7:9-11; 11:7, 8.

Riddle: A question designed to test the mental agility and ingenuity of the audience. Matthew 11:11; Mark 2:19: 7:15; 8:27; John 2:19.

Sarcasm: (literally "flesh-tearing") is the blatant use of apparent praise for dispraise. It is less direct than invective in that it employs inversion as a means of deflection so that its sting is a little more indirect. Matthew 9:12, 13.

Satire: A work or manner that blends a censorious attitude with humour and wit for improving human institutions or

Forms of Humour (with examples from the Gospels)

humanity. Satirists attempt through laughter not so much to tear down as to inspire remodeling. Satirists are often personally involved with the objects of criticism and realize that their proposed remedy must not be seen by the audience as more repulsive than the disease. Luke 7:24–28.

Simile: A figure in which a similarity between two objects is directly expressed by the use of 'like' or 'as.' Matthew 10:16; 23:27.

Travesty: When a weighty subject is addressed in a lesser style (opposite of parody). Matthew 11:16–19; Luke 7:31–34.

Appendix B
Definitions of Wonder (Imagination and Creativity)

"The world of the imagination is a world of unborn or embryonic beliefs: if you believe what you read in literature, you can, quite literally, believe anything."

—Northrop Frye

"Imagination implies the ability to imagine – to make things up. The imagination is not limited to observable reality."

—Leland Ryken

"'World-making' is a prime activity of the artistic imagination. . . . And there is mystery in the imagination: It transcends the limitations of external reality in a manner that seems magical."

—Leland Ryken.

"The imagination . . . plays the game of make-believe. It simplifies and heightens reality. It is a more highly structured world than the one we live in."

—Leland Ryken.

"Imagination in its proper meaning is never an addition, it is an evocation. It is perception, not piquancy [provocation]. Its work is not cosmetical or decorative; it is a function of percipiency [perception]. It is exercised not only in the perception of new qualities in

Definitions of Wonder (Imagination and Creativity)

things, but also in the discovery of hitherto unseen relationships between things...."

—Joseph Sittler.

"... creativity results from the interaction of a system composed of three elements: a culture that sustains symbolic rules, a person who brings novelty into the symbolic domain, and a field of experts who recognize and validate the innovation. All three are necessary for a creative idea, product, or discovery to take place."

—Mihaly Csikszentmihalyi

"Creativity is the generation of unique, innovative thoughts, actions, and feelings, with appropriate implementation for the benefit of others. It often means little more than the ability of perceiving in an unhabitual way. It is a function of knowledge, imagination, and evaluation."

—Howard Hendricks

"Imagination is the mental tool we have for connecting material and spiritual, visible and invisible, earth and heaven."

—Eugene Peterson

"Imagination fuels and feeds creativity. Imagination is a vision of possibilities. Imagination is the capacity to see."

—David Larsen.

"Imagination is conjuring up inside one, by use of a very special intellectual muscle, that which is absent or elusive, by making it concrete."

—Frederick Buechner

"Imagination and logic may be understood as two ways of thinking, or as two qualities of thought that are, to some extent, mutually dependent. Logic is unidirectional or linear, moving step-by-step to a specific purpose or intent. It finds meaningful connections between ideas primarily on a temporal axis of cause and effect. By contrast, imagination finds a meaningful connection between two apparently dissimilar ideas that have no causal relationship."

—Paul Scott Wilson.

Appendix B

"Imagination of this kind is the true germ of faith; it is the power of conceiving as definite the things which are invisible to the senses, - of giving them distinct shape. And this, not merely in your own thoughts, but with the power of presenting the things which experience cannot primarily teach to other people's minds, so that they shall be as just as obvious as though seen with the bodily eye."
—Henry Ward Beecher.

"Creativity refers to the invention or origination of any new thing (a product, solution, artwork, literary work, joke, etc.) that has value."
—Wikipedia

"Imagination, also called the faculty of imagining, is the ability of forming new images and sensations when they are not perceived through sight, hearing, or other senses."
—Wikipedia

Appendix C
Comparison of Left-Mode and Right-Mode Characteristics of the Brain[1]

LEFT MODE	RIGHT MODE
Verbal: Using words to name, describe, define.	*Nonverbal:* Awareness of things, but minimal connection with words.
Analytic: Figuring things out step by step and part by part.	*Synthetic:* Putting things together to form wholes.
Symbolic: Using a symbol to stand for something (e.g., the + sign stands for the process of addition.	*Concrete:* Relating to things as they are at the present moment.
Abstract: Taking out a small bit of information and using it to represent the whole thing.	*Analogic:* Seeing likenesses between things; understanding metaphoric relationships, comparisons.
Temporal: Keeping track of time, sequencing one thing after another. Doing first things first, second things second.	*Nontemporal:* Without a sense of time.
Rational: Drawing conclusions based on reason and facts.	*Nonrational:* Not requiring a basis of reason or facts; willingness to suspend judgment.
Digital: Using numbers, as in counting.	*Spatial:* Seeing where things are in relation to other things and how parts go together to form a whole.

1. Howard Hendricks, *Color Outside the Lines*, 43.

Appendix C

LEFT MODE	RIGHT MODE
Logical: Drawing conclusions based on logic: one thing following another (e.g., mathematical theorem or a well-stated argument).	*Intuitive:* Making leaps of insight often based on incomplete patterns, hunches, feelings, or visual images.
Linear: Thinking in terms of linked ideas, one thought directly following another, often leading to a convergent conclusion.	*Holistic:* Seeing whole things all at once; perceiving the overall patterns and structures, often leading to divergent conclusions.

Bibliography

Abrams, M.H. *A Glossary of Literary Terms*, 7th ed. Boston, MA: Heinle and Heinle, 1999.
Achtemeier, Elizabeth. *Creative Preaching: Finding the Words*. Nashville, TN: Abingdon Press, 1980.
Aristotle. *The Rhetoric and Poetics of Aristotle*. Trans. by W.W. Roberts and I. Bywater. New York, NY: Modern Library, 1954.
Arthurs, Jeffrey D. *Preaching with Variety*. Grand Rapids, MI: Kregel, 2007.
Banting, Blayne A. "Proclaiming the Messiah's Mirth: A Rhetorico-contextual Model for the Interpretation and Proclamation of Humour in Selected Gospel Sayings." D.Min. thesis, Acadia Divinity College, 1998.
———. *Take Up and Preach: A Primer for Interpreting Preaching Texts*. Longwood, FL: Xulon Press, 2010.
Barth, Karl. *Ethics*. Trans. by Geoffrey Bromiley. New York, NY: Seabury Press, 1981.
———. *Portrait of Karl Barth*. Trans. by Robert McAffee Brown and George Casalis. Garden City, NY: Doubleday, 1963.
———. *The Doctrine of Creation*. III.I Church Dogmatics. Edinburgh, UK: T and T Clark, 1958.
———. *The Doctrine of Creation*. III.4 Church Dogmatics. Edinburgh, UK: T and T Clark, 1961.
———. *The Doctrine of God*. II.I Church Dogmatics. Edinburgh, UK: T and T Clark, 1957.
Beasley-Murray, George R. *Jesus and the Kingdom of God*. Grand Rapids, MI: Eerdmans, 1986.
Berger, Peter. *A Rumour of Angels*, Garden City, NY: Doubleday and Company, 1969.
Bergquist, Carlisle. "A Comparative View of Creativity Theories: Psychoanalytic, Behavioristic, and Humanistic." http://www.vantagequest.org/trees/comparative.htm.
Beukema, John. "Why Serious Preachers Use Humor." In *The Art and Craft of Biblical Preaching*, edited by Haddon Robinson and Craig Brian Larson, 130–40. Grand Rapids, MI: Zondervan, 2005.

Bibliography

Blais, Donald. "Wisdom as Trickster: Jesus the Christ and Mary the Queen of Heaven as Trickster Archetypes." Boston: MA: Tri-regional Meeting of the American Academy of Religion, 1995.

Buechner, Frederick. *Telling the Truth: The Gospel as Tragedy, Comedy and Fairy Tale.* New York, NY: Harper and Row, 1977.

Borg, Marcus. *Jesus: A New Vision.* San Francisco, CA: Harper, 1987.

Boyd, George. *Cynic, Sage, or Son of God?* Wheaton, IL: Bridgepoint Books, 1995.

Brueggemann, Walter. *The Prophetic Imagination.* Philadelphia, PA: Fortress Press, 1978.

Bullard, John Moore. "Biblical Humor: Its Nature and Function." Ph.D. diss., Yale University, 1962.

Cameron, Julie. *Finding Water: The Art of Perseverance.* New York, NY: Jeremy P. Tarcher/Penguin, 2006.

———. *The Artist's Way: A Spiritual Path to Higher Creativity.* New York, NY: G.P. Putnam's Sons, 1992.

———. *Walking in This World: The Practical Art of Creativity.* New York, NY: Jeremy P. Tarcher/Putnam, 2002.

Carroll, R.P. "Is Humour Also Among the Prophets?" In *On Humour and the Comic in the Hebrew Bible,* edited by Yehuda T. Radday, and Athalya Brenner, 169–89. Sheffield, UK: Almond Press, 1990.

Carson, D.A. *The Gospel According to John.* Grand Rapids, MI: Eerdmans, 1991.

Childers, Jana. *Performing the Word: Preaching as Theatre.* Nashville, TN: Abingdon Press, 1998.

——— and Clayton J. Schmit, eds. *Performance in Preaching: Bringing the Sermon to Life.* Grand Rapids, MI: Baker, 2008.

Cousins, Norman. *Anatomy of an Illness.* 19th ed. New York, NY: W.W. Norton, 1981.

Cox, Harvey. *The Feast of Fools.* Cambridge, MA: Harvard University Press, 1969.

Critchley, Simon. *On Humour.* London, UK: Routledge, 2002.

Csikszentmihalyi, Mihaly. *Creativity.* New York, NY: HarperCollins, 1996.

de Bono, Edward. *Serious Creativity.* New York, NY: HarperCollins, 1992.

Downing, F. G. *Cynics and Christian Origins.* Edinburgh, UK: Clark, 1992.

Drakeford, John W. *Humor in Preaching.* Grand Rapids, MI: Zondervan, 1986.

Edwards, Michael. "The World Could Not Contain the Books." In *The Bible as Rhetoric,* edited by Martin Warner. London, UK: Routledge, 1990.

Elliot, J.K., ed. *The Apocryphal New Testament.* Oxford, UK: Clarendon Press, 1993.

Erickson, Millard J. *Christian Theology.* Grand Rapids, MI: Baker, 1983.

———. *Concise Dictionary of Christian Theology.* Grand Rapids, MI: Baker, 1984.

Feist, Gregory J. "A Meta-analysis of the Impact of Personality on Scientific and Artistic Creativity." *Personality and Social Psychological Review* 2 (1998) 290–309.

Bibliography

Frye, Northrop. *The Educated Imagination*. Toronto, ON: Anansi, 1963.
———. *The Great Code: The Bible and Literature*. New York, NY: Harcourt, Brace and Jovanovich, 1982.
———. "The Nature of Satire." In *Satire: Theory and Practice*, edited by Charles A. Allen and George D. Stevens. Belmont, CA: Wadsworth, 1962.
Gabora, Liane. "Creativity." https://people.ok.ubc.ca/lgabora/research.htm# Creativity.
Gadamer, Hans Georg. *Truth and Method*. Trans. by Garrett Barden and John Cumming. New York, NY: Seabury, 1975.
Galli, Mark and Craig Brian Larson. *Preaching That Connects*. Grand Rapids, MI: Zondervan, 1994.
Good, Edwin M. *Irony in the Old Testament*. Sheffield, UK: Almond Press, 1981.
Grenz, Stanley J. *Theology for the Community of God*. Nashville, TN: Broadman and Holman, 1994.
Guilford, J.P. *The Nature of Human Intelligence*. New York, NY: McGraw-Hill, 1967.
Harpur, Tom. *The Pagan Christ*. New York, NY: Walker and Company, 2004.
Hoefler, Richard Carl. *Creative Preaching and Oral Writing*. Lima, OH: CSS Publishing, 1978.
Howard. J. Grant. *Creativity in Preaching*. Grand Rapids, MI: Zondervan, 1987.
Howard, Robert. "Technology and the Sermon." In *The New Interpreter's Handbook of Preaching*, edited by Paul Scott Wilson, 366–68. Nashville, TN: Abingdon Press, 2008.
Huizinga, Johan. *Homo Ludens. A Study of the Play Element in Culture*. London, UK: Temple Smith, 1949.
Hyers, Conrad, ed. *Holy Laughter: Essays on Religion in the Comic Perspective*. New York, NY: Seabury, 1969.
———. *The Comic Vision and the Christian Faith*. New York, NY: Pilgrim Press, 1981.
———. *The Meaning of Creation*. Atlanta, GA: John Knox Press, 1984.
Irenaeus of Lyons. *Against the Heresies*. Trans. by Dominic J. Unger. New York, NY: Paulist Press, 1992.
Jacobson, Rolf A., ed. *Crazy Talk: A Not-So-Stuffy Dictionary of Theological Terms*. Minneapolis, MN: Augsburg, 2008.
Johnson, Luke Timothy. *The Real Jesus*. San Francisco, CA: Harper, 1995.
Johnston, Robert K. *The Christian at Play*. Grand Rapids, MI: Eerdmans, 1983.
Jonsson, Jakob. *Humour and Irony in the New Testament Illustrated by Parallels in Talmud and Midrash*. Beihefte Der Zeitschrift Fur Religions-Und Geistesgeschichte. Leiden, NL: E.J. Brill, 1985.
Kant, Immanuel. *The Critique of Judgment*. Trans. By J.C. Meredith. Oxford, UK: Clarendon Press, 1952.
Keen, Sam. *Apology for Wonder*. New York, NY: Harper and Row, 1969.
Keller, Timothy J. *Center Church*. Grand Rapids, MI: Zondervan, 2012.
Koestler, Arthur. *The Act of Creation*. London, UK: Penguin, 1964.

Bibliography

Kozbelt, Aaron, et al. "Theories of Creativity." In *The Cambridge Handbook of Creativity*, Edited by James C. Kaufman and Robert J. Sternberg, 20–47. Cambridge, UK: Cambridge University Press, 2010.

Kuschel, Karl-Josef. *Laughter. A Theological Reflection*. New York, NY: Continuum, 1994.

Langan, Janine. "The Christian Imagination." In *The Christian Imagination*, edited by Leland Ryken. 63–80. Colorado Springs, CO: Shaw Books, 2002.

Larsen, David L. *Telling the Old, Old Story: The Art of Narrative Preaching*. Wheaton, IL: Crossway Books, 1995.

L'Engle, Madeline. *Walking on Water: Reflections on Faith and Art*. New York, NY: Bantam, 1980.

Lehrer, Jonah. *Imagine. How Creativity Works*. Toronto, ON: Allen Lane, 2012.

Martin, Rod A. *The Psychology of Humor. An Integrative Approach*. Burlington, ON: Academic Press, 2007.

Mead, Peter. *Biblical Preaching* (blog). http://wordpress.com/.

Migliore, Daniel L. "Karl Barth: Theologian with a Sense of Humor." *The Princeton Seminary Bulletin* (1986) 276–80.

Miller, David. *Gods and Games*. New York, NY: Harper and Row, 1973.

Moltmann, Jürgen. *Theology of Play*. New York, NY: Harper and Row, 1972.

Montifiore, C.G. and H. Loewe, eds. *A Rabbinic Anthology*. New York, NY: Schlocken Books, 1974.

Motyer, Alec. *Look to the Rock: An Old Testament Background to Our Understanding of Christ*. Leicester, UK: InterVarsity Press, 1996.

Newman, Marc C. "Video Clips." In *The New Interpreter's Handbook of Preaching*, edited by Paul Scott Wilson, 209–10. Nashville, TN: Abingdon Press, 2008.

Nickerson, R.S. "Enhancing Creativity." In *Handbook of Creativity*, edited by R.J. Sternberg, 392–430. Cambridge, UK: Cambridge University Press, 1999.

Niebuhr, Reinhold, "Humour and Faith." In *Holy Laughter*, edited by Conrad Hyers, 134–49. New York, NY: Seabury Press, 1969.

Nilson, Don L.F. *Humor Scholarship*. Westport, CT: Greenwood Press, 1993.

O'Brien, Peter T. *Colossians, Philemon*. Word Biblical Commentary. 44. Waco, TX: Word, 1982.

Oden, Thomas. *The Living God*. New York, NY: Harper and Row, 1987.

Peterson, Eugene H. *Eat This Book: A Conversation in the Art of Spiritual Reading*. Grand Rapids, MI: Eerdmans, 2006.

———. *Under the Unpredictable Plant: An Exploration in Vocational Holiness*. Grand Rapids, MI: Eerdmans, 1994.

Plucker, Jonathan A., and Matthew C. Makel. "Assessment of Creativity." In *Cambridge Handbook of Creativity*, edited by James C. Kaufman and Robert J. Sternberg, 48–73. Cambridge, UK: Cambridge University Press, 2010.

Radday, Yehuda T. and Athalya Brenner, eds. *On Humour and the Comic in the Hebrew Bible*. Sheffield, UK: Almond Press, 1990.

Bibliography

Rahner, Hugo. *Man at Play*. Trans. by Brian Battershaw and Edward Quinn. New York, NY: Herder and Herder, 1967.

Ramsey, Thor. *A Comedian's Guide to Theology*. Ventura, CA: Regal Books, 2008.

Russ, Sandra W., and Julie A. Fiorelli. "Developmental Approaches to Creativity." In *Cambridge Handbook of Creativity*, edited by James C. Kaufman and Robert J. Sternberg, 233–49. Cambridge, UK: Cambridge University Press, 2010.

Ryken, Leland. *The Liberated Imagination: Thinking Christianly About the Arts*. Wheaton, IL: Harold Shaw, 1989.

Sayers, Dorothy L. *The Whimsical Christian*. New York, NY: Macmillan 1978.

Schultze, Quentin J. "Technology." In *The New Interpreter's Handbook of Preaching*, edited by Paul Scott Wilson, 332–36. Nashville, TN: Abingdon Press, 2008.

Schwarz, Christian A. *Natural Church Development: A Guide to Eight Essential Qualities of Healthy Churches*. St. Charles, IL: ChurchSmart Resources, 1996.

Skinner, Craig. "Creativity in Preaching." In *Handbook of Contemporary Preaching*, edited by Michael Duduit, 562–70. Nashville, TN: Broadman Press, 1992.

Sternberg, R.J. and T.I. Lubarti. "The Concept of Creativity: Prospects and Paradigms." In *Handbook of Creativity*, edited by R.J. Sternberg, 3–15. Cambridge, UK: Cambridge University Press, 1999.

Stevens, R. Paul. *The Other Six Days: Vocation, Work, and Ministry in Biblical Perspective*. Grand Rapids, MI: Eerdmans, 1999.

Tozer, A.W. "The Value of a Sanctified Imagination." In *Developing a Christian Imagination*, edited by Warren W. Wiersbe, 211–14. Wheaton, IL: Victor Books, 1995.

Troeger, Thomas, H. "Imagination/Creativity." In *The New Interpreter's Handbook of Preaching*, edited by Paul Scott Wilson, 191–92. Nashville, TN: Abingdon Press, 2008.

———. *Imagining a Sermon*. Nashville, TN: Abingdon Press, 1990.

Von Oech, Roger. *A Kick in the Seat of the Pants*. New York, NY: Harper and Row, 1986.

———. *A Whack on the Side of the Head*. 3rd ed. New York, NY: Business Plus, 2008.

Wallas, Graham. *The Art of Thought*. New York, NY: Harcourt, Brace and Company, 1926.

Webb, Joseph M. *Comedy and Preaching*. St. Louis, MO: Chalice Press, 1998.

Whedbee, J. William. *The Bible and the Comic Vision*. Cambridge, UK: Cambridge University Press, 1998.

Wiersbe, Warren W. *Developing a Christian Imagination: An Interpretive Anthology*. Wheaton, IL: VictorBooks, 1995.

Bibliography

———. "Imagination: The Preacher's Neglected Ally." In *The Art and Craft of Biblical Preaching*, edited by Haddon Robinson and Craig Brian Larson, 562–66. Grand Rapids, MI: Zondervan, 2005.

———. *Preaching and Teaching with Imagination: The Quest for Biblical Ministry*. Wheaton, IL: Victor Books, 1994.

Willimon, William H. "Humor." In *Concise Encyclopedia of Preaching*, edited by William H. Willimon and Richard Lischer, 262–64. Louisville, KY: Westminster John Knox Press, 1995.

———. *Peculiar Speech: Preaching to the Baptized*. Grand Rapids, MI: Eerdmans, 1992.

Wilson, Paul Scott. "Beyond Narrative: Imagination in the Sermon." In *Listening to the Word. Studies in Honor of Fred B. Craddock*, edited by Gail R. O'Day and Thomas G. Long, 131–46. Nashville, TN: Abingdon Press, 1993.

———. *Imagination of the Heart: New Understandings in Preaching*. Nashville, TN: Abingdon Press, 1988.

———. "Imagination." In *Concise Encyclopedia of Preaching*, edited by William H. Willimon and Richard Lischer, 266–69. Louisville, KY: Westminster John Knox Press, 1995.

www.ingramcontent.com/pod-product-compliance
Lightning Source LLC
Chambersburg PA
CBHW072145160426
43197CB00012B/2254